Henry James and the Requirements
of the Imagination

Henry James and the Requirements of the Imagination

PHILIP M. WEINSTEIN

Harvard University Press
Cambridge, Massachusetts
1971

© Copyright 1971 by the President and Fellows of Harvard College

All rights reserved

Distributed in Great Britain by Oxford University Press, London

Publication of this book has been aided by a grant from the Hyder Edward Rollins Fund

Library of Congress Catalog Card Number 74-158430

SBN 674-38785-6

Printed in the United States of America

Preface

I‌T I‌S A P‌LEASURE—probably the only unalloyed pleasure connected with the writing of this book—to acknowledge those
people who have made my own work possible. To Laurence
Holland's unforgettable lectures at Princeton I owe an interest
in James that, after ten years of dormancy, has finally found
its own expression. To the example of Lawrance Thompson,
in class at Princeton and out, I owe my conviction that only
a teacher full of life himself can make literature come alive.

Monroe Engel, who read this study in an earlier form, has
been unstinting in his kindness and in the proffering of advice
that freed rather than intimidated me. And Reuben Brower,
through his attention both to my prose and to my argument,
has taught me that grace and a wrought clarity are not the
ornaments but the index of serious literary criticism.

Finally, to my wife Penny, who has sustained both this work
and its author, my debt is greatest.

P. M. W.

September 1970
Cambridge, Massachusetts

Contents

Henry James and the Requirements of the Imagination

The artist is present in every page of every book from which he sought so assiduously to eliminate himself.

Henry James

I shall get just the good I said a few moments ago I wished to put into Isabel's reach—that of having met the requirements of my imagination.

The Portrait of a Lady

There was the difference and the opposition, as I really believe I was already aware—that one way of taking life was to go in for everything and everyone, which kept you abundantly occupied; and the other was to be as occupied, quite as occupied, just with the sense and the image of it all, and on only a fifth of the actual immersion: a circumstance extremely strange.

Henry James, Autobiography

Introduction

Like walking, criticism is a pretty nearly universal art; both require a constant intricate shifting and catching of balance; neither can be questioned much in process; and few perform either really well.

R. P. Blackmur, "A Critic's Job of Work"

WHEN, AS A SOPHOMORE IN COLLEGE, I first came into contact with the work of Henry James, I chanced to read him at his best. I read *The Ambassadors,* and I still remember the unexpected blend of elation and perplexity that made up my response. The elation derived from my sense of the liberating enrichment of life Strether gains in Paris, an enrichment that seems to fulfill his exhortation to little Bilham: "Live all you can!" At the same time my perplexity came from gradually realizing that Strether somehow betrays his own advice and fails to "live all he can," that the kind of living he finally exemplifies, with its sacrifices and deprivations, contrasts fundamentally, if obscurely, with what he urges upon little Bilham.

That initial elation and perplexity concerning James, though never again so distinct, has remained with me, and this book can best be seen as an attempt to understand and elaborate the complex adventure of Lambert Strether. To make sense of the space between his advice and his example, between "living" as he urges it and "living" as he embodies it, is to

1

interpret one of the chief paradoxes in James's fiction: the "tension between the impulse to plunge into 'experience' and the impulse to renounce it."[1] If I could see in what ways my two responses to Strether's drama were related, were in fact two halves of an inclusive response, I could then interpret the paradox and give my own comprehensive reading of what "living" means in James. Such a reading is the aim of this book.

What Strether urges upon little Bilham, with all of its ramifications, I refer to as "experience." The term is admittedly vague, and I use it with different emphases as it means different things in James's work. Many of them, however, are implied in Strether's outburst: the encounter with European civilization (the fullness of a sensuous life and a living intellectual community lacking in Woollett); the possession of a casual expertise, manifested by Chad and his circle; the attainment of intimacy and passion, implied by Chad's very bearing; and, most comprehensively, the sense of having realized one's potential identity through active immersion in the world. These concerns, in one form or another, are present in James's fictive world from *Roderick Hudson* to *The Golden Bowl*. They define, for his innocent heroes, the domain of genuine experience, the fully achieved life.

The faculty in Strether which sees Chad in such a way as to prompt his famous words to little Bilham, and yet which subtly prevents him from living according to those words, is something that, with all of *its* ramifications, I refer to as "imagination," the protean interior vision that so largely shapes the behavior of the Jamesian hero. In its multiple facets—artistic, idealistic, innocent, vicarious, obsessive—the imagination is explored by James throughout his work. It is the peculiar interaction between this subjective energy and the outside world that directs—when it does not actually constitute—the essential ac-

1. Philip Rahv, "Attitudes Toward Henry James," in *The Question of Henry James: A Collection of Critical Essays,* ed. F. W. Dupee (New York: Holt, 1945), p. 278.

tivity in James's fiction. In other words, the exercise of the imagination on the part of James's characters plays an extra-ordinary role in molding the kinds of experience they undergo. In the following chapters I attempt to define extensively the nature of this interplay.

Because James is so concerned with the behavior of the imagination, because a character's private speculations tend to take the place of any intimate or passionate relationship with others, because the crucial moments are often like Isabel Archer's sitting alone, "motionlessly seeing," there is a forceful analogy between the activity of the novelist himself, solitary but creative, and the activity typically engaged in by the characters within his work. Although I base no interpretation of the fiction upon James's biography, ample internal evidence throughout the novels suggests that James did explore the unique moral implications attaching to the life of the artist. There may be, he implies again and again, something suspect about the vocation itself. In my chapter on *The Sacred Fount,* where the internal evidence seems irresistible, I make such a case.

The novels most important for my reading are *The Portrait of a Lady* and *The Ambassadors,* but in *Roderick Hudson,* with its different artists and its imaginative princess, my themes first take definite shape. There the two modes of living—vision and action—are roughly embodied in separate characters, Rowland and Roderick, and this early novel serves as a prepa-ration for *The Portrait of a Lady,* where the contrasting modes are uneasily blended in Isabel Archer. She is consequently a character of rich, various, and confusing traits, and my detailed chapter on *The Portrait,* like that on *The Ambassadors,* at-tempts to relate the final act of self-restraint to the earlier goal of self-fulfillment.

To bridge the gap between *The Portrait of a Lady* and the novels of the nineties, I have devoted several pages to some of the formal changes—as they influence my themes—that occur in James's fiction after the theater debacle. *What Maisie Knew* and *The Sacred Fount* can then be approached as groundwork for a more inclusive reading of *The Ambassadors*. As extreme products of a particular line of development, these two short novels illuminate one of the directions James had been moving in ever since *Roderick Hudson*. Together they clarify much that is bewildering in *The Portrait of a Lady* and enable *The Ambassadors* to stand as not only a masterpiece in its own right but as the triumphant expression of interests and forms that had begun to appear a quarter of a century earlier.

In conclusion, I had no choice but to come to grips with *The Golden Bowl,* James's final and massive attempt to fuse the imaginative life with the life of passional experience. In this most difficult and ambiguous of novels, James attempts to express the successful union of those modes of living that I have argued in each chapter to be fundamentally irreconcilable. For reasons that have been gathering throughout his career, such a resolution, I find, is not only strained but unconvincing, even appalling.

The terrain I am exploring is, of course, not *terra incognita*. As early as 1934, Edmund Wilson, in a brilliant and seminal essay, probed "the ambiguity of Henry James," and the relation between imagination and experience that I trace in these pages unapologetically follows along kindred lines. Well before Wilson's essay appeared, W. C. Brownell delivered a devastating critique of James's work, and, in 1925, Van Wyck Brooks magisterially, if indiscriminately, addressed himself to the weaknesses in the novels. Only recently, taking his cue from Brooks, Maxwell Geismar has attempted, in a massively shrewd if carping and self-indulgent book, to remake the case against James. In all these instances, through brevity, failure to attend to the novels themselves, or intemperate "overkill," a critical but sympathetic reading of the ambiguous nature of imagination and experience in James's work has been suggested but not accomplished.[2]

There are many competent critics of Henry James, and three in particular have proved indispensable to my work. F. W. Dupee's brief biography still strikes me as a rare combination of grace, insight, and comprehensive judgment. R. P. Blackmur's varied and pithy essays on James remain inexhaustibly suggestive; one can only wonder at the interest his projected volume on James would have had. Laurence Holland's *The Expense of Vision*, though more generous to the fiction than I am able to be, both crystallized my own thinking about James and served as a model for the serious criticism of a literary genre. Beyond my indebtedness to these three writers, I owe a general debt to Leon Edel that no would-be critic of Henry James can fail to incur. His contributions to Jamesian scholarship have reached that magnitude where disagreement with some of his conclusions becomes almost superfluous; he himself often presents us with the materials we use to dispute his readings. Oscar Cargill's massive summation of Jamesian scholarship and F. O. Matthiessen's various contributions to Jamesiana—the novelist's family, his later novels, his notebooks—proved invaluable. Richard Poirier's work on the early James and Marius Bewley's and Tony Tanner's work on the later fiction have substantially influenced my own reading of the same novels, and my debt to them, whether in agreement or disagreement, is considerable.[3]

2. Edmund Wilson, "The Ambiguity of Henry James," *The Triple Thinkers*, rev. ed. (New York: Oxford University Press, 1963), pp. 88–132; W. C. Brownell, "Henry James," in *American Prose Masters* (New York: Scribner's, 1909), pp. 339–400; Van Wyck Brooks, *The Pilgrimage of Henry James* (New York: Dutton, 1925); Maxwell Geismar, *Henry James and the Jacobites* (Boston: Houghton Mifflin, 1963).
3. F. W. Dupee, *Henry James*, rev. ed. (New York: Dell, 1956); Laurence B. Holland, *The Expense of Vision: Essays on the Craft of Henry James* (Princeton, N.J.: Princeton University Press, 1964). R. P. Blackmur's ten or twelve pieces on James are scattered throughout various journals and anthologies. Several appear as introductions to the

This study came within an inch of being entitled *Open Windows and Closed Doors,* but at the last moment a metaphor that might sound coy was sacrificed for a descriptive title that, if less provocative, is also less ambiguous. Nevertheless, the metaphor penetrates deeply into the world of James's novels, and the reader will find it used recurrently as an organizing frame of reference. The contrast to which it points is quite simple. Windows are customarily seen through; doors walked through. With some figurative extension, the open windows are meant to signify the multifold visions, the expansive panoramas so characteristic of the Jamesian hero's imagination, while the closed doors suggest the fate of a certain kind of experience in James's world: the stifled nature of intimate or passionate relationships that, balked, either do not come to fruition, or do so only behind closed doors. Both phrases recur, literally, in several of the novels; metaphorically, they convey the shape of that vision of life which I find at the center of James's fictive world.

A few words are in order about the way I go about the work of criticism. In each of the six chapters I quote extensively from the text, focusing on those facets of form and theme that most persuasively convey the particular drama I am attempting to make salient. My method is frankly eclectic. To delineate the living structure of each novel—precisely those luminous but undefined elements which first made me choose this novel rather than another—is the principle loosely behind

---

Dell paperback editions of the novels. The others can be located in Maurice Beebe and William T. Stafford, "Criticism of Henry James: A Selected Checklist," *Modern Fiction Studies,* 12 (Spring 1966), 117–177. Leon Edel's and F. O. Matthiessen's volumes on James are too numerous and well known to need mention here. Richard Poirier, *The Comic Sense of Henry James: A Study of the Early Novels* (New York: Oxford University Press, 1960); Oscar Cargill, *The Novels of Henry James* (New York: Macmillan, 1961); Marius Bewley, *The Complex Fate* (London: Chatto and Windus, 1952); Tony Tanner, "Henry James," in *The Reign of Wonder: Naivety and Reality in American Literature* (New York: Cambridge University Press, 1965), pp. 259–335.

my readings. If the reader senses a subjective and recurrent emphasis on a certain locale within the larger Jamesian domain, I can only answer that literary criticism is always in large part subjective and that to my mind this is the essential Henry James. Though the critic's honor depends upon the questioning and "objectifying" process to which he submits his insights, to forgo those insights invites even deeper peril.

If my reading of the six selected novels proves persuasive, its application to James's other work will be apparent. I have chosen those books where the conflict between imagination and experience seems to me most acute and interesting, with some stress on the later fiction. There are other novels relevant to my interests: *The American, The Princess Casamassima, The Spoils of Poynton,* and *The Wings of the Dove,* not to mention a host of short stories. Nevertheless, this study is as long as it needs to be; either the main lines from *Roderick Hudson* to *The Golden Bowl* are drawn convincingly or they are not. One last remark: if the tone of my argument seems at times harsh or petulant or unduly faultfinding, it is nevertheless true that this book could not have been undertaken without a deep-seated response to its subject.

I   The Romantic and the Real: Beliefs and Roles in *Roderick Hudson*

My subject, all blissfully . . . had defined itself—and this in spite of the title of the book—as not directly, in the least, my young sculptor's adventure. This it had been but indirectly, being all the while in essence . . . his friend's and patron's view and experience of him.

Preface to Roderick Hudson

. . . but what I resent is that the range of your vision should pretend to be the limit of my action.

Roderick Hudson

"THE REAL REPRESENTS TO MY PERCEPTION the things we cannot possibly *not* know," James wrote in his 1907 Preface to *The American,* and one way of approaching *Roderick Hudson* is to see it as a deliberate and thoroughgoing immersion into the meager conditions of "the real."[1] The romantic wish fulfillment that eludes authorial judgment in the conclusion of *Watch and Ward* is both recognized and comprehensively taken to task in this second novel. In the place of Roger Lawrence's mild achievement we find a triple study in aspiration and failure.

A young man embodying the myth of the fiery romantic

1. Henry James, *The Art of the Novel,* ed. R. P. Blackmur (New York: Scribner's, 1934), p. 31.

genius, a woman seeking to find and believe in "what you call in Boston one's higher self,"[2] and a slightly older man who believes both in the essential "salubrity of genius"(292) and, as a guideline for his own role, the perfect fusion of "moral and aesthetic curiosity"(16)—these are the "cases" James explores in his first successful novel. Different though they be, Roderick, Christina, and Rowland all share the goal of self-realization. Disgruntled with their present selves, they want—through artistic creation, a deeper encounter with European culture, heightened personal interrelationships—to develop into that ideal image of themselves, that sought-after identity in which "one's weary imagination at last may rest"(260).

This goal virtually obsesses James throughout his career, and in *Roderick Hudson* he begins to treat it with his characteristic complexity. Ideal self-realization is shown to be at once admirable and impossible, a moral odyssey and a sentimental pipedream. Moreover, the process of self-realization is paradoxical, involving altruism as well as exploitation, beginning as an exploration of untapped energies and ending as an imprisonment within stale roles. As such, this novel presents in simplified miniature the essential Jamesian paradigm: inflation followed by deflation; *illusions* followed by *illusions perdues*. In *Roderick Hudson* this paradigm may be best explored as it is expressed through a series of optimistic beliefs, beliefs first cherished, then challenged, and finally betrayed. Because the destiny of these beliefs coincides with the destiny of the major characters, this chapter explores the gospel of living by focusing on the drama of belief: the search for something or someone to believe in, and the testing of beliefs already held.

Of the three leading characters Roderick is surely the least convincing as a novelistic creation, the one with whom, interest-

2. Henry James, *Roderick Hudson* (New York: Scribner's, 1907), p. 263. Subsequent quotations from *Roderick* refer to this edition (Volume I of the New York Ed.); hereafter, all page references will be incorporated within the text, parenthetically, after the quotation.

ingly, James has the most trouble. The sculptor seldom escapes sufficiently from his literary heritage to generate the illusion of life. His name suggests Roderick Usher, and Poe seems to have been in James's mind when Roderick recounts to Rowland his melodramatic parting from Striker: "Allow me to put these [books] back in their places. I shall never have need for them more—never more, never more, never more!"(46). In addition, his fate—precocious genius, stormy emotional life, violent early death—echoes faithfully the cliché pattern of romantic Shelleyan genius. From his first entry at Cecilia's he does "everything too fast"(20); he seeks audaciously to create "a magnificent image of my Native Land"(118); he intends to work only at the level of pure inspiration. In his trajectory he embodies the bankruptcy of an extreme version of romanticism: the problem of what to do and how to live between the intermittent flashes of vision. There is hardly space, given my focus, to demonstrate how, through Roderick, James is exploring the tenets of a nineteenth-century romantic myth of creativity. But it is interesting to note in passing that a poetics founded on pure, untutored inspiration and originality is accompanied by an obsessive concern with the passage from the creative innocence and wonder of childhood to the sterile and customary perspectives of adult experience. The visionary moments come less often and less powerfully until finally, somewhat like Wordsworth in the "Immortality Ode," Roderick will wonder if the ideal exists in this life at all: "I don't know how early he [Stendhal] saw it; I saw it before I was born—in another state of being. I can't describe it positively; I can only say I don't find it anywhere now"(273).

Soon after his introduction as "a remarkably pretty boy"(17), Roderick's high voice, chronic passivity, and incurably melodramatic tone begin insistently to suggest a state of arrested adolescence. Like a child, he would rather fly than learn to walk. His death comes from stumbling over an Alpine cliff, thus rendering prophetic Gloriani's criticism of the statue of the drinking youth: "Your beauty . . . is the effort of a man to quit the earth by flapping his arms very hard. He may jump about or stand on tiptoe, but he can't do more. Here you jump about very gracefully, I admit; but you can't fly; there's no use trying"(119). Unwilling to walk and incapable of flight, Roderick echoes once more the Shelleyan dilemma: "Oh, lift me as a wave, a leaf, a cloud! / I fall upon the thorns of life! I bleed!"

In addition to showing the collapse of Roderick's romantic genius, James explores the blindness and the egotism that accompany the sculptor's gift. Throughout his whirlwind initiation into the great civilized world, Roderick rarely deviates from an exploitation of others that, in its massive naïveté, can only be called infantile. Exclaiming to Rowland that "you demand of us to be imaginative, and you deny us the things that feed the imagination"(224), the sculptor proceeds to reject all limitation or choice whatsoever. Thus, while pursuing Christina, it never occurs to him to break off with Mary.

Moreover, though he protests on behalf of a large imagination, Roderick's is often narrow and occasionally coarse. He seems oddly not to recognize himself as the cause of the "interesting" changes in his mother's face: "Oh, I don't suppose it represents the trace of orgies! But whatever it is, mammy, it's a great improvement; it makes you a very good face . . . It has two or three rare tragic lines in it; something might be done with it"(331). Charged with abusively misunderstanding his benefactor, ignoring his fiancée, and meanly judging Christina, Roderick, after Rowland's eruption, is finally penitent: "I've been damnably stupid. Isn't an artist supposed to be a man of fine perceptions? I haven't, as it turns out, had *one*"(512).

Because this self-condemnation rings true and because Roderick's egotism attains superhuman proportions, it is difficult to respond fully to his imputed imaginative power, so vitiated is that power by moral and other shortcomings. Consequently, it becomes difficult for the reader to accept Rowland's faith in Roderick as a romantic genius. James enlarges the difficulty by often imprisoning his sculptor within a hyperbolic ranting idiom from which he periodically emerges to strike the reader as a rather beautiful, innocent, and exasperating child.

Indeed, after he is finally informed of Rowland's suppressed feelings for Mary, the detached candor of Roderick's remarks approaches the sublime: "But I never dreamed you were in love with her. It's a pity that she doesn't care for you." When Rowland admits that he hopes she may someday be moved, Roderick replies: "Well, I don't believe it, you know. She idolises me, and if she never were to see me again she would idolise my memory"(511).

More frequently, however, Roderick's theatrical tone and simplistic judgments prevent his being taken seriously by the reader, as when he criticizes Christina to Rowland and his mother: "She led me to believe that she would send her Prince about his business and keep herself free and sacred and pure for me . . . It turned my head, and I lived only to see my happiness come to pass. She did everything to encourage me to hope it would; everything her infernal coquetry and falsity could suggest"(429). There is further self-pitying attitudinizing in his lament to Rowland near Lake Como: "Pity me, my friend, pity me! Look at this lovely world and think what it must be to be dead to it! . . . Dead, dead; dead and buried! Buried in an open grave where you lie staring up at the sailing clouds, smelling the waving flowers and hearing all nature live and grow above you"(466). The mixture of inflation, distortion, and posturing in such phrases and gestures gives a melodramatic quality to the detail of Roderick's life that corresponds to the larger melodrama of his hackneyed and conventional destiny.

James usually controls Roderick's theatricality and exploits it for thematic purposes. For example, Rowland responds dead-

pan to Roderick's tirade ("Dead, dead; dead and buried!"):
"I'm very glad to hear it. Death of that sort's very near to
resurrection"(466). One may feel, nonetheless, that such in-
flated language often goes further than "placing" Roderick;
it serves unintentionally to undermine belief in him altogether.
As F. W. Dupee surmises, "In Roderick's gigantic sculptures,
his exploits in the Coliseum, his spectacular death in the Alps,
James was being romantic about romanticism."[3] With regard
to the "exploits in the Coliseum," however, I shall later argue
that James knew exactly what he was doing.

Still, in his presentation of Roderick, James's blend of satire
and sympathy—and, within the satire, of effective irony and
lifeless cliché—exacts upon the novel a severe cost. Roderick
Hudson is not a sufficiently credible character, his career does
not ultimately convince, and the relationships in the book that
depend on a critical belief in him are correspondingly impaired.[4] Of course, the primary subject, as James himself recognized years later in the Preface to the New York Edition
of *Roderick Hudson,* is not "the young sculptor's adventure,"
but rather "his friend's and patron's view and experience of
him."[5] This stress on Rowland not only salvages the novel,
but it is also of the greatest significance in indicating, as early
as 1875, the kind of character and the kind of experience that
James's imaginative genius would, during the next thirty years,
most successfully depict.

What James embodies in Roderick, then, is a mélange of
several conflicting and abiding feelings about aesthetics and
morality, romantic self-realization and realistic limits. Imaginative genius is accompanied by blind, exploitative egotism, and

3. F. W. Dupee, *Henry James,* rev. ed. (New York: Dell, 1956),
p. 74.
4. It is a moot point as to how critically James wanted the reader
to "take" Roderick. Nevertheless, he presumably did not mean to discredit
the sculptor altogether; and my interpretation is probably more severe
than James intended. Despite his flaws, Roderick seems designed as a
tragic figure, but I do not find him credible enough to attain this status.
5. James, *Art of the Novel,* p. 15.

13

romantic aspiration is intertwined with the language and gestures of sentimental melodrama. The creative imagination, as seen in Roderick, is incommensurate with the moral, responsible life, and the devotion to idealistic art—witnessed through his first creation, the innocent youth—seems doomed to failure. Further speculation about these oppositions seems unprofitable since, in delineating Roderick, James has failed to create a character convincing enough to "reward" the questions one wants to ask about him. In fact, James's confused attitudes toward "the Roderick figure" create within the sculptor contradictions sufficient to destroy him, and the youth who begins his romantic drama by crying to Rowland, "Upon my soul, you *believe* in me!"(35) will listlessly end it by commenting, again to Rowland, about the giant shadow cast by Singleton: "He's like me, he'll have passed for ten minutes for bigger than he is"(482).

If Roderick embodies one kind of belief that the novel ruthlessly scrutinizes, Christina Light's subtler, more elusive drama comes more clearly into focus as a quest for another kind of belief. Appearing abruptly and unheralded with her entourage of the Cavaliere, Mrs. Light, and the fantastic poodle "decked like a ram for sacrifice," she has "the step and carriage of a tired princess"(95), and seems as fabulous as a creature emerging from a Spenserian pageant. Disdain and boredom, "the reserve of systematic indifference"(151), appear to be her characteristic responses to life.

As the reader learns more of her makeshift and biased education, however, he becomes aware of her immense loathing both for that education and for her mother's vulgarity. When, for example, Roderick proposes to do a bust of Christina and Mrs. Light expresses some reluctance, her daughter coolly explains: "Mamma hesitates . . . because she doesn't know whether you mean she shall pay you for the bust or you'll pay me for the sitting. She's capable of thinking of *that*, mamma. I can assure you at least that she won't pay you a sou"(158).

Educated to esteem nothing but wealth and titles, Christina, recoiling, has developed an erratic contempt for materialism, for the great social world in whose standards her mother devoutly believes. Yet, despite herself, Christina has been "educated": "I'm fond of luxury, I'm fond of a great society, I'm fond of being looked at, I thrill with the idea of high consideration. Mamma, you see, has never had *any*. There I am in all my native horror. I'm corrupt, corrupting, corruption!"(407).

A tone of self-disgust seems often to crop up under Christina's urbane cynicism. And it rises to the surface when she wittily, if feverishly, proclaims to Rowland that she, for her part, appreciates Mary Garland:

"I do her justice. I do her full justice." She wonderfully kept it up. "I like to say that, I like to be able to say it. She's full of intelligence and courage and devotion. She doesn't do me a grain of justice; but that's no harm—I mean above all no harm to *her*. There's something so noble in the aversions of a good woman! . . . I should like to have a friendship with her . . . But I shan't have one now—not if she can help it! . . . It's fatality—that's what they call it, isn't it? We make the most inconvenient good impression on people we don't care for; we inspire with loathing those we do. But I appreciate her, I do her justice; that's the most important thing. It's because I've after all a lot of imagination. She has none. Never mind; it's her only fault. Besides, imagination's not a virtue—it's a vice. I do her justice; I understand very well"[381].

The breathless rhythms; the desire to "do Mary justice," both in her own eyes and in Rowland's; the melodramatically imagined situation; the mingled self-laceration, self-pity, and self-justification; the praise for Mary Garland that becomes increasingly suspect in its frenetic emphasis, as well as in the involuntary jab ("She has none"); the implied parallel complaint that Rowland also loathes her while admiring Mary;

15

and the barely concealed jealousy toward Mary for having inspired his belief where she failed—all of these elements flicker through that speech to convey Christina's engaging complexity.

Poignant though the passage is, it is also neatly turned and somewhat self-conscious, and it is Christina's fate to be incapable of convincing others of her sincerity. As Madame Grandoni succinctly puts it, "she cries as naturally as possible"(196). Rowland's first impression had been that "she was playing a part before the world"(153–154); and a glint of artifice lurks in all her gestures, as when she asks Rowland, after an apparently intimate scene, to give his opinion of her now: "Ah, this pressed the spring, and his inward irony, for himself, gave a hum! . . . She had played her great scene, she had made her point, and now she had her eye at the hole in the curtain and she was watching the house"(410).

Christina's various performances, while unfailingly picturesque, nevertheless strike Rowland "as an easy use of her imagination . . . But it was no disfiguring mask, since she herself was evidently the foremost dupe of her inventions. She had a fictitious history in which she believed much more fondly than in her real one . . . She liked to carry herself further and further, to see herself in situation and action"(278). One gathers, from such a passage, that an intolerable home life has caused Christina to flee, as it were, to the stage, and that by creating illusory roles she can ignore the real one her mother has been at such pains to prepare. Throughout his career James remains fascinated with those characters whose unrestrained imaginations create "fictitious histories." Here, as in *The Portrait of a Lady, The Sacred Fount,* and *The Ambassadors,* he explores the motives for creating such "histories" and the various consequences of believing in them. But in Christina's case the other roles fail to convince, and when she pleads with Rowland, "You don't believe in me! not a grain! I don't know what I wouldn't give to *force* you to believe in me!"(310), her words vibrate with her own self-doubt.

What she seeks in her various roles is an inviolable, credible identity that meets the requirements of her active imagination. Failing this, she would seek to immerse herself in someone else's sustaining integrity: "I'm tired to death of myself; I would give all I possess to get out of myself; but somehow at the end I find myself so vastly more interesting than nine-tenths of the people I meet"(208). With this understanding of her in mind, we are able to see that Christina's affair with Roderick possesses a certain inevitability, as a close examination of their scene in the Coliseum will reveal.

Surrounded by this decaying edifice consecrated to former heroic endeavor, Christina finds it all too easy to measure Roderick's shortcomings: "you're simply as weak as any other *petit jeune homme*. I'm so sorry! I hoped—I really believed—you were strong"(259). When Roderick protests against the unfairness of this charge, Christina coolly grants his point and goes on to say that the cause of his failure is immaterial, "so long as it keeps you from splendid achievement. Is it written then that I shall really never know what I've so often dreamed of?"(259). Undeterred by such rhetorical posturing, Roderick asks what her dream may be:

"A man whom I can have the luxury of respecting!" cried the girl with a sudden flame. "A man whom I can admire enough to make me know I'm doing it . . . In such a man as that, I say, one's weary imagination at last may rest"[259–260].

Christina wants a hero, and the flamboyant sculptor had appealed vividly. But, as in the climax to Keats's most haunting poems, his life cannot possibly satisfy the requirements of her dream: "Your voice, at any rate, *caro mio,* condemns you; I always wondered at it; it's not the voice of a conqueror!"(261). In the enormous Coliseum these words reverberate; conquerors are of an earlier epoch; what is there to "conquer" in the latter part of the nineteenth century? Poor Roderick can only feebly come back with "Give me something

17

to conquer," whereupon Christina reveals what a modern conqueror might do:

> You've never chosen, I say; you've been afraid to choose. You've never really looked in the face the fact that you're false, that you've broken your faith. You've never looked at it and seen that it was hideous and yet said "No matter, I'll brave the penalty, I'll bear the shame." You've closed your eyes, you've tried to stifle remembrance . . . You've faltered and dodged and drifted, you've gone on from accident to accident, and I'm sure that at this present moment you can't tell what it is you really wish [262].

Christina charges that Roderick, amoral egotist that he is, lacks the courage to confront and confirm his own behavior. Society for her being a tangled skein of pettiness and vulgar rapacity, she seeks in her hero absolute, transcendent self-assertion, something like a "Superman." Such a hero would allow Christina the "luxury" of respect; he "should really give me a certain feeling" (261). The egotistic frivolity in these phrases renders the beginning of her next attack unintentionally ironic:

> You're one of the men who care only for themselves and for what they can make of themselves. That's very well when they can make something great, and I could interest myself in a man of extraordinary power who should wish to turn all his passions to account. But if the power should turn out to be, after all, rather ordinary? Fancy feeling one's self ground in the mill of a third-rate talent![262].[6]

Since he lacks the intrepidity to abide by heroic choices, according to Christina, Roderick also lacks form—design—in

---

6. At this point, as we reflect on the condition of her interest in Roderick (that he turn "all his passions to account"), an earlier, enigmatic speech of Christina's becomes more significant: "Tell me this: do you think he's going to be a *real* swell, a *big* celebrity, have his life written, make his fortune, and immortalise—as the real ones *do,* you know—the people he has done busts of and the women he has loved?" (212).

his life and, consequently, in his art. He is not purposive enough "to turn his passions to account." The amoral character of Roderick's speeches about the creative imagination now reappears in the anarchic thoughts of Christina. Heroism, she implies, attaches less to one's positive achievements than to the destruction one can cause, the social conventions one is bold enough to defy in the journey toward self-fulfillment. Christina will say to Rowland at a later point: " '*Il n'est ni banal ni bête;* and then there's nothing in life he's afraid of. He's not afraid of failure; he's not afraid of ruin or death.' Rowland had a stare—he indeed had a chill—for this singular description. 'Oh, he's a romantic figure!' " (408).

This essentially "chilling," life-denying view of heroism, or romance, is displayed in acts of mere recklessness and negation (*"n'est . . . ni . . . ni . . .* nothing . . . not . . . not . . ."*), and poor Roderick can assert himself in the Coliseum in only one way: to risk his life for a flower. The goal may be intrinsically petty, but the heroism resides in the magnitude of the risk; again the storied Coliseum diminishes this gesture by placing it within an appropriate context.

Christina's most revealing remark, however, is her fear of "feeling one's self ground in the mill of a third-rate talent!" Desiring her life to be a heroic adventure, Christina sees herself as a priceless entity, to be bestowed only upon a man who embodies that finer integrity her imagination is in search of. Roderick, it follows, is unacceptable because, in not turning all his passions to account, he will fail, finally, to turn *her* passions to account. The giving of herself will not result in a formed or significant experience, an act of art or life; she will have bungled her "chance" for life, and she is too valuable to be thus wasted, to be ground in the mill of a third-rate talent.

The irony, of course, is that a third-rate melodrama, complete with illegitimate child, will shatter her romance. In consenting to marry the Prince, she foregoes the grand opportunity of her dreams and accepts a role in which there is no possibility of self-belief. Cynicism is an easy outlet, and she takes it, loathing equally herself and the society that tricked her. Hereafter, one may hazard, she will respond most deeply to a coarse, unfeeling masculinity that values her as little as she does herself and thus meets her need for self-humiliation.[7]

Similarly, her interest in Rowland Mallet—nowhere explicit but everywhere implied—is furthered by nothing so much as his resistance of her charms. Perhaps perversely attracted to him, she nevertheless has the clear-eyed ability to recognize something heroic in Rowland's self-restraint and partially to pattern her own (temporary) rejection of the Prince on Rowland's example of "the better self." The peculiar stresses and even indignities attaching to that example of "the better self"—the uncomfortable role of Rowland Mallet—are what we need next to consider.

Any discussion of the scene in the Coliseum is incomplete without reference to the curious position of Rowland Mallet, eavesdropper, passive spectator, *deus ex machina.* Indulging his enjoyment of the picturesque Coliseum—much as his elder counterpart, Lambert Strether, will relish an artful Lambinet-like landscape—Rowland abruptly breaks off his romantic reverie to attend to a more urgent interchange between Christina and Roderick. Though Rowland is restricted to mere spectatorship and the inference or imagination of intimacy rather than actual participation in it, his position in the Coliseum—above the actors and unseen by them—suggests a watchful god or stage manager. When matters get out of hand and his "character" is about to risk his life, Rowland promptly descends, like Shakespeare's "Duke of dark corners," "and the next moment

7. In scanning *Roderick Hudson* as a preparation for writing *The Princess Casamassima,* James seems to have been struck by just this trait in Christina, as he elaborates it in her later *faible* for Paul Muniment. This and other matters connected with Christina's reappearance in *The Princess Casamassima* are perceptively dealt with by M. E. Grenander, "Henry James's *Capricciosa,*" *PMLA,* 65 (June 1960), 309–319.

a stronger pair of hands than Christina's were laid upon Roderick's shoulders"(265–266).

The least charitable view of Rowland's ambivalent role is conveyed by his own self-recriminating phrase, "a meddlesome donkey"(292), in a letter to Cecilia. A fairer judgment in the same letter is more relevant: "Without flattering myself I may say that I'm cursed with sympathy—I mean as an active faculty"(293). No artist himself, Rowland yet has the artist's sympathetic imagination.

At no other point, one may remark, are the two heroes—and the poles of romanticism they reflect—so far apart, as a later description of Roderick's genius makes abundantly clear: "The great and characteristic point with him was the perfect separateness of his sensibility. He never saw himself as part of a whole; only as the clear-cut, sharp-edged, isolated individual, rejoicing or raging . . . but needing in any case absolutely to affirm himself"(429). Rowland, on the other hand, enters vicariously into the lives of those around him, seeking to help them realize to the full their potential. It is, of course, a potential measured by his own limited imagination: the gesture of liberation is at the same time one of restriction, and Roderick resents "that the range of your vision should pretend to be the limit of my action"(504).

As early as the second page of the book we are told that Rowland chafed at seeing "a bright proud woman [Cecilia] live in such a small dull way"(2). The first chapter is full of his uneasy sense of uselessness, of talk about devoting himself to some project or other:

I'm tired of myself, my own thoughts, my own affairs, my own eternal company. True happiness, we are told, consists in getting out of one's self . . . and to stay out you must have some absorbing errand . . . I want to care for something or for somebody. And I want to care, don't you see? with a certain intensity; even, if you can believe it, with a certain passion. I can't just now be intense and passionate about a hospital or a dormitory [7–8].

21

Thwarted, like Christina Light, and unsure of his identity, neither "irresponsibly contemplative" nor "sturdily practical," Rowland finds in Roderick Hudson the solution to his own problem. Cultivating Roderick will at once meet both his aesthetic and his moral requirements. Through Roderick's success he will be vicariously fulfilled. The parasitic elements in Rowland's "design" must be neither exaggerated nor obscured. The fugitive artist in Rowland, technically unskilled, finds his material in human beings; by mediating Roderick's development and later Mary Garland's, Rowland's artistic instinct obliquely satisfies itself. But the breadth and selflessness of his vision for others, the sincerity of his interest, attest to Rowland's idealism and disqualify any simplistic view of him. He is deeply altruistic; he is also deeply implicated.

Rowland's belief in Roderick, though it temporarily kindles life in the sculptor, is built upon fatally inadequate tenets. To put it simply, Rowland's imagination naively assumes in Roderick his own moral qualities, plus creative genius. There is no awareness of payments to be made, of deficiencies in one realm exacted by excesses in another; Rowland's timid artistic imagination is balanced with a vengeance by Roderick's callow moral imagination. Assuming that their views of experience naturally coincide, Rowland has no qualms about letting Roderick loose in Rome, and Roderick wastes little time before informing Rowland "that he meant to live freely and largely and be as interested as occasion demanded. Rowland saw no reason to regard this as a menace of undue surrender to the senses, because in the first place there was in almost any crudity of 'pleasure,' refine upon it as the imagination might, a vulgar side which would disqualify it for Roderick's favour"(92).

After the first debauch in Switzerland, Rowland is aghast:

During the long stretch of their comradeship Roderick had shown so little impatience to see what was vulgarly called life that he [Rowland] had come to think of that possibility as a cancelled danger . . . What right had a man who was engaged to that delightful girl in Northampton to behave as if his consciousness were a common blank, to be filled in with coarse sensations? Yes, distinctly, he had lost an illusion, an illusion that he had loved[136–137].

"Crudity," "vulgar," "what is vulgarly called life," "common," "coarse"—these words make clear to the reader just how fastidious Rowland's concept of experience is.

Although Rowland's imagination is incapable of assessing Roderick, it is perceptive in areas where Roderick's imagination is blind. Though uncreative, Rowland is tirelessly observant; he sees in Mary Garland and in Christina Light potentialities and depths of meaning wholly obscure to the sculptor. Cursed or gifted with sympathy as an active faculty, like his creator, Rowland guesses the unseen from the seen, senses that Mary is herself a "case," and, from a few clues, is able to reconstruct Christina's paternity and the torment she has undergone. Yet his imagination is not all sufficient, for Christina's interest in him would never have been divined if Roderick had not blurted it out; and, more damagingly, his view of Mary, so much finer and more intrinsically interesting than Roderick's, turns out to be unjustified.

With regard to Mary he is far from disinterested, and this takes us back to the initial ambivalence of his role. Both self-implicated and selfless in his commitment to Roderick's career, Rowland cannot view that career with detachment; nor can he see Mary as other than the ideal wife he wants but is destined not to have, whose self-development in Rome is in part objectively realized and in part subjectively desired. His is a false role, since "meddling" with Roderick's future can only be justified by clean hands, and his feeling for Mary destroys this possibility.

The ensuing stress between desire and intention ennobles Rowland; "it's what a man is meant for"(50). But it strains him beyond the breaking point, and the fractures reveal themselves in various ways. Most disfiguring is his temptation to remain passive and reap the results of Roderick's failure. After his "agony in the garden" at Fiesole, this temptation is repulsed, but it reappears in subtler form at the end of the book. Without quite admitting it to himself, Rowland makes love to Mary as they travel from Florence to Switzerland; their flower scene reenacts the somewhat puerile heroics of the lovers in the Coliseum and unmistakably suggests Rowland's essay at Roderick's role.

Constantly Mary's gestures are overinterpreted. Alternately sulking and exulting, Rowland reads into them Roderick's fall and his own gradual replacement in her esteem. He comes finally to see Mary as developed so far beyond Roderick's deserving that, when he is intolerably taunted, Rowland commits the Jamesian heresy of sounding off, of letting go, of shifting his burden to Roderick's neophyte conscience—a burden that Roderick cannot bear. At the sight of the sculptor's dead body, Mary's all revealing gesture and "loud tremendous cry" (526) shatter for good the "palace of thought" that Rowland's biased imagination had so carefully and lovingly constructed. His dreams of fulfillment are ended. Belief in Roderick, an idealized image of Mary, a role for himself that can accommodate his aesthetic and moral requirements—all have been exposed as illusory.[8] Given the ambivalence of his role at the beginning, it is perhaps inevitable that, though patient and not cynical, Rowland should be left with nothing.

8. Rowland faces up to his loss: "But if one was to believe in you as I've done one was to pay a tax on one's faith!" (508). Singleton, however, cannot bear to give up his illusion. Through the strange requirements of his own imagination, the painter has come to endow Roderick with those idealized, heroic traits the latter sought to express in his sculpture: "Don't tell me! I want to know no evil of him . . . In my memories of this Roman artist life he will be the central figure. He will stand there in extraordinary high relief, as beautiful and clear and complete as one of his own statues!" (415–416). Roderick, in an obscure way, is too important to Singleton to be given up merely because he was false; Singleton converts the sculptor into a work of art just as Strether will later convert Madame de Vionnet into the genius of French civilization.

Now that we have seen how several of the beliefs and myths of self-realization are scrutinized or deflated in *Roderick Hudson,* we can focus on the ways in which the disillusionment is conveyed and the world of severe limitations introduced. In moving his characters from the assumption of infinite choice to the knowledge of inescapable restrictions, James has recourse to several motifs, themes, and metaphors which express, here and throughout his fiction, the processes of reduction. We might well begin with James's treatment of the fairy tale.

"Coming here all unannounced, unknown, so rich and so polite, and carrying off . . . [Roderick] in a golden cloud"(65), Rowland strikes Mary Garland and the two Hudsons as a fairy godfather. It all seems "so much like a fairy-tale," the one requirement being (and no one gives this a second thought): "You've only to work hard"(37). The words themselves are beautifully ambivalent. For Roderick they prove the reality of the fairy tale; for the reader on his second time around, who hears quite another tone, they belie it. In the early stages of the book, however, the fairy tale suggests limitless self-development, and it is an appropriate context for the budding genius on the brink of his career.

Several months and disillusioning experiences later, however, Rowland begins to squirm at the implications of his role; after all, "he had not undertaken to make him over"(173). The squirming only intensifies when the worried yet trustful Mrs. Hudson, now in Rome, reassures herself by telling Rowland, "You're our guardian angel; it's what Mary and I call you"(329). When the situation finally becomes clarified, the new configuration of roles has sinister implications; the fairy godfather, proven defective, has been transformed into the scapegoat: "she [Mrs. Hudson] found it infinitely comfortable to lay the burden of their common affliction upon Rowland's broad shoulders. Had he not promised to make them all rich and happy? And this was the end of it!"(432-433). Not only are fairy tales seen to be expensive illusions, suggesting unreal

25

options, but the impossibility of reactivating Roderick is described in terms of them: "An essential spring had dried up within him, and there was no household magic, no waving of any blest wand, to make it flow again"(444–445).

Rather than accommodating his own desires, Rowland's role as guardian angel has become ultimately imprisoning. Caught within its confines when things go wrong, he has no choice but, as scapegoat, to pay with a frozen, immovable grin. He is exploited constantly by Mrs. Hudson: "she would have thought him cruelly recreant if he had suddenly turned his back, and yet she gave him no visible credit for consistency. It often struck him that he had too abjectly forfeited his freedom"(447).

His prescribed role is even more constricting in relation to Mary, for he is acutely uncomfortable whenever he attempts to deviate from it into something closer to a lover's stance. As a result he remains frustrated, condemned to be Mary's companion and never more than that. On the last page of the book we are told of the journey back to Northampton, "made of course with his assistance," during which "she had used him, with the last rigour of consistency, as a character definitely appointed to her use." Thus Rowland is reduced even beyond the role of scapegoat, from stage manager to lackey.

In different ways the same imprisoning effect can be detected in the roles played by Mary, Christina, and Roderick. Mary, described at first as always sewing or knitting some coarse domestic object, appears in Rome as "older, easier, lighter; she had . . . more form . . . It was like something she had been working at in the long days of home, an exquisite embroidery or a careful compilation, and she now presented the whole wealth of it as a kind of pious offering"(324). This perfectly prepared metaphor of rich and artful self-development, of having carefully made of herself "an exquisite embroidery," leads the reader to imagine Mary as having a "case" of her own, and one watches with interest her incipient struggle with

Northampton angularities. Yet the outcome—Mary's cry and her residing with Mrs. Hudson—betrays this pattern of growth and reasserts her inescapable role: the bleak New England woman, patiently sewing herself into spinsterhood. As with Catherine Sloper at the end of *Washington Square,* an essential spring has been tampered with, and the door to further experience is closed.

With Christina, the pattern of fixity underlying apparent freedom to develop is even more salient; again and again she essays a role, regards herself searchingly "in situation and in action," seeking a destiny in which she can realize "what you call in Boston one's higher self." Yet, all along, her tawdry, melodramatic role has been waiting in abeyance; she is an illegitimate daughter of the Cavaliere, and, once this definition has been revealed to her, there is no escaping its confines. Her identity is not achieved but "disclosed," and in cynical revulsion she gives up her struggle to create an acceptable role: "Happiness? I mean to cultivate delight"(492).

To discuss Roderick in these terms requires only a slight shift in focus from character traits to life-style. Although he seeks a life of total freedom as a creative artist, Roderick is nevertheless imprisoned within the narrow possibilities of his own compulsive, melodramatic style. He is what Richard Poirier in his fine chapter on *Roderick Hudson* calls a fixed character, comic and incapable of growth.[9] His habits of feeling and responding limit his options so effectually that plummeting over an Alpine cliff can be seen as the inevitable dénouement of a career already rigorously characterized by clichés of thinking and acting.

Not only do the characters find themselves imprisoned within their roles, either tricked by or robbed of their ideals; they also come to distrust the more worldly goals they began by sharing. Experience becomes a dangerous and elusive term; Rowland finds that Roderick means by it something more sen-

9. Richard Poirier, *The Comic Sense of Henry James: A Study of the Early Novels* (New York: Oxford University Press, 1960), pp. 11–43.

sual and vulgar than his own fastidious appreciation of European culture. Roderick finds, moreover, that experience, as *he* sought it, has devastated his fragile talent and left him, like Rowland, with nothing.

As a corollary, passion, too, is revealed as a compromising and corrupting agent. The question for Mary Garland, as later for May Server and Marie de Vionnet, is how abject, how self-humiliating will she turn out to have been: "Was she one of those who would *be* abject for some last scrap of the feast of their dream?"(444). Roderick has been destroyed by his uncontrolled, egocentric passions; conversely, Rowland is surely meant to be admired for his arduous attempt to restrain his feeling for Mary.

Beyond these particular observations, some basic tropes in *Roderick Hudson* express James's deep-seated ideas about the nature of self-realization and self-restraint. As many critics have noted, the image of the cup of experience runs throughout his work; it first appears in this novel as Roderick's sculpture of "thirst," and it recurs in conjunction with his Paterian "appetite for novelty . . . he was eating his cake all at once and might have none left for the morrow"(89–90). Later we hear Roderick discourse on genius itself as something "dealt out in different doses . . . we drink them down in the dark and we can't tell their size until we tip them up and hear the last gurgle"(230).

As the novel enters the phase of disillusionment, the contents of the cup turn sour; we find Rowland "fairly used to his daily dose of bitterness, and after a hard look, as always, at the cup, he again swallowed the draught and entered, responsively and formally, into Mrs. Hudson's dilemma"(434). No longer a fairy tale promising limitless self-fulfillment, his experience has become an agony of self-waste or self-restraint: "Rowland suddenly felt the cup of his own ordeal full to overflowing, and his long-gathered bitterness surged into the simple clear passion of pain at wasted kindness"(506).

In thus surrendering for the first time to the temptation to let go, to tell Roderick what he thinks of him, Rowland commits a blunder which, we are made to feel, he will always regret. Less conspicuous, then, than the figure of draining the cup of experience, but even more significant in James's fictive world are the various metaphors of *holding on*, of (to borrow Joyce's figure) bearing one's chalice through the streets. Far from signifying the expansive, self-fulfilling encounter with life, the rich and open experiencing of life, these metaphors, which are buried in *Roderick Hudson* and the rest of James's fiction, suggest the value of self-restraint, of self-preservation, even of self-hoarding. Again and again Rowland is on the verge of throwing up his hands or cursing, but he nearly always manages to restrain himself. To Roderick he says, "If you've got facility, respect it, nurse it, adore it, save it up in an old stocking—don't speculate on it"(140). As with Christina in the Coliseum scene, we are dealing with a rare and precious value to be expended only in supreme moments. The image reappears when Rowland sees Mary's richer features in Rome: "it was beautifully as if this expression had been accumulating all the while, lacking on the scene of her life any channel to waste itself"(324).

Whether the characters are prodigal or chary, then, the great disaster is waste, and, using the same figure, James can suggest with poignancy the waste of Roderick's life: "On the whole, and most of the time, he irresistibly appealed, the air being charged with him as with some rich wasted essence, some spirit scattered by the breaking of its phial and yet unable, for its very quality, to lose itself"(446). One is only days away, at this point, from Roderick's final dissolution, when he will, in his own prediction, "disappear, dissolve, be carried off in a something as pretty, let us hope, as the drifted spray of a fountain"(231).

One final figure of disillusionment brings this chapter to a close. Quite early in the book Rowland characterized himself to Cecilia as "a man of genius half-finished," lacking genius but needing expression, and thus spending his days "groping for the latch of a closed door"(8). Later, the same image is expanded to describe a plea for youthful flexibility: "They say that old people do find themselves at last face to face with a solid blank wall and stand thumping against it in vain. It resounds, it seems to have something beyond it, but it won't move. That's only a reason for living with open doors as long as we can"(88). Here the figure of the open door connotes the ideal life of unrestricted self-development and rich personal interrelationships. Significantly, then, the most poignant failure in the book, the one which the others but echo, is the failure of Rowland to maintain faith in Roderick, and it is first decisively described in these terms:

Rowland meditated a moment. "Are your fatalism and your folly prepared to lose you the best friend you have?"
Roderick looked up; he still smiled. "I defy them to rid me—!"
His best friend clapped on that gentleman's hat and strode away; in a moment the door sharply closed[306].

II The Drama of "Motionlessly Seeing":
The Portrait of a Lady

Her imagination was by nature ridiculously active; when the door was not open it jumped out of the window.

The Portrait of a Lady

. . . what is truer than that on one side—the side of their independence of flood and field, of the moving accident, of battle and murder and sudden death—her adventures are to be mild? Without her sense of them, her sense for them, as one may say, they are next to nothing at all; but isn't the beauty and the difficulty just in showing their mystic conversion by that sense, conversion into the stuff of drama or, even more delightful word still, of "story"?

Preface to The Portrait of a Lady

IF THE GRAND ASPIRATIONS ENTERTAINED in *Roderick Hudson* can be seen to culminate in the figure of a closed door, Isabel Archer finds, during her famous meditative scene, that "the infinite vista of a multiplied life" has become "a dark, narrow alley with a dead wall at the end."[1] In his Preface to the novel written some twenty-five years later, James considered this scene "obviously the best thing in the book," the

1. Henry James, *The Portrait of a Lady* (New York: Scribner's, 1908), II,189. Subsequent quotations from *The Portrait* refer to this edition (Volumes III and IV of the New York Ed.); hereafter, all page references will be included within the text, parenthetically, after the quotation.

supreme justification of the "interesting and . . . beautiful . . . difficulty" of constructing an entire novel around the consciousness of a mere woman. Removing peripheral concerns—such as "comic relief and underplots . . . murders and battles and the great mutations of the world"—James wants to "show what an 'exciting' inward life may do for the person leading it even while it remains perfectly normal." For illustration he goes unhesitatingly to the scene where Isabel, all alone, sits by her dying fire far into the night. "It is a representation simply of her motionlessly *seeing,* and an attempt withal to make the mere still lucidity of her act as 'interesting' as the surprise of a caravan or the identification of a pirate . . . it all goes on without her being approached by another person and without her leaving her chair."[2]

James's obvious delight in this chapter emphasizes the importance he attached to the experience of "motionlessly seeing," and Charles Anderson, among other critics, has indicated the myriad ways in which chapter xlii effortlessly pulls together the main motifs of the novel.[3] The reader, however, may find something not only bold but also fastidious in this chapter and in James's emphasis upon it, something that renders the scene an apt *point de départ* for talking about the experience of Isabel Archer. What is bold is the defiance of literary convention implied in James's refusal simply to marry Isabel off or to make her tangential to a series of larger, exciting concerns—as Shakespeare did with Portia and Cleopatra—which might buoy her up should her own intrinsic "case" fail of interest. Rather than being bound to a ready-made fate dictated by convention, Isabel appears first to her creator as an "unattached character" of rich and undetermined potential, "a cer-

2. Henry James, *The Art of the Novel,* ed. R. P. Blackmur (New York: Scribner's, 1934), pp. 57, 51, 50, 56–57, 57.

3. Charles R. Anderson, "Person, Place, and Thing in James's *The Portrait of a Lady,*" in *Essays on American Literature in Honor of Jay B. Hubbell,* ed. Clarence Gohdes (Durham, N.C.: Duke University Press, 1967), pp. 164–182.

tain young woman affronting her destiny." Isabel is to create her own story, and Ralph Touchett will have occasion to reflect: "Most women did with themselves nothing at all; they waited, in attitudes more or less gracefully passive, for a man to come that way and furnish them with a destiny. Isabel's originality was that she gave one an impression of having intentions of her own"(I,87). The author's "primary question" in the Preface, is "Well, what will she *do?*" And, as James makes amply clear, nothing that she does is richer and more portentous than her sitting alone, "motionlessly seeing."[4]

What replaces a more conventional view of experience—"murders and battles and the great mutations of the world"—betrays, however, a certain fastidiousness. Events seen in the mind and reflected upon, anticipated, imagined, or remembered, assume a greater burden of importance, here and throughout James's fiction, than the actual events themselves. What one does often matters less than what one sees, or perhaps it is better to say that, in James's fiction, seeing tends to replace doing, *is* doing. This points to a range of experience increasingly free of action in the grosser sense of "things being done" and to a possible tendency, while always prizing experience, to see mere action as increasingly gross.

This contrast between seeing and doing, so subtle and deceptive in *The Portrait,* virtually jumps out at the reader in *Roderick Hudson.* "I make the beastly mistakes, and you find the proper names for them"(481), Roderick angrily snaps at Rowland. His words cast light on the peculiar passivity of the older man and suggest that special relationship between an author and his created character—where one person sees, even shapes, what another does—that James seems so often to have in mind as an analogue for relationships *within* his fiction. This analogue is discussed later in connection with *The Portrait,* as well as in my chapters on *The Sacred Fount, The Ambassadors,* and *The Golden Bowl.*

4. James, *Art of the Novel,* pp. 44, 48, 53.

Moreover, as I suggested in my first chapter, James's greater success with the passive, observing character—the Rowland rather than the Roderick figure—strongly suggests the shape his fiction will take. For one thing, intimacy between men and women is usually inaccessible to the observing character, and it is rarely described directly in James's work; the focus is rather on a person's relation to himself or on his vicarious reconstruction of other people's relations. Rowland Mallet's experience was seen to be largely of this nature, and one of the aims of my study is to demonstrate that such experience—of which Isabel's "motionlessly seeing" is another example—tends to precede all others.

Immediately some interesting corollaries follow. In this kind of experience nothing conventionally momentous need happen and no more than one figure—the observer himself—need intimately participate. Moreover, the link between the imagination of an event and the event itself is extremely flexible. Through imagination it is possible to reconstruct events as they actually occurred. Or one may, at a distance and through refined intuitional and perceptual powers, come to grasp the latent and profound meaning of events that eludes the actual participants themselves. What is just as likely in James's fictive world, however, is that the imaginative construct "improves" upon or even seriously distorts actuality. Finally, of course, as Shakespeare warns in *A Midsummer Night's Dream:* "The lunatic, the lover, and the poet / Are of imagination all compact," and one may imaginatively "create" events that never took place at all.

Such mental experience, with its stress upon imagination and its requiring no more than a single individual, is essentially analogous to the vicarious experience of the author himself as he creates his various fictions. The implications of such an "artistic" version of experience are explored throughout this work; in my chapter on *The Sacred Fount* they are the paramount concern. At this point I need only suggest that the relation between the biography and the fiction becomes intimate in a curious way. That is, it is not so much a question of James's incorporating into his art this known character or that particular experience, but of his incorporating a personal stance toward the entirety of experience.

In this connection, Joseph Warren Beach astutely describes one of the links between James's art and his life. After a study of the *Notebooks,* Beach is struck with "the essential loneliness of James, his comparative want of commitment to intimate personal relations of the kind that require an absolute surrender of one's self to the demands of 'life' . . . No one touched life at more points, but he seems to have touched it with the imagination, at a distance, with a steady maintenance of esthetic detachment . . . There is something pathetic in James's reference to his own intensities of 'living' in the seclusion of his workshop—living, that is, in the passionate reconstruction of the lives of imaginary beings."[5] It should be clear, in the following pages, that I am not interpreting the novels in the light of James's specific biography, but that I am exploring parallels between the typical activity of his fictive world and what I take to be certain generic characteristics of the act of literary creation.

In the case of *The Portrait,* Isabel's "extraordinary meditative vigil" is presented as one of her most intense adventures; the more "expected" scenes of emotion and intimacy—her union with Osmond, her increasingly horrified glimpses into his real character, the birth and death of her baby—are passed over without mention in the four-year break between chapters xxxv and xxxvi. In James's work such scenes are either reflected through someone's memory of them or reconstructed through someone's imagination of them (either that of the characters or of the reader). This illuminates what I have called the element of fastidiousness present in the experience that takes place in the novel, an experience located primarily in the con-

5. Joseph Warren Beach, "The Witness of the Notebooks," in *Forms of Modern Fiction,* ed. William Van O'Conner (Minneapolis: University of Minnesota Press, 1948), p. 48.

sciousness or imagination of Isabel rather than in a direct depiction of the intimate encounters themselves.

By focusing on the imaginative or remembering mind, James increasingly refrains from a close description of *what* is being imagined or remembered, and he thus creates for himself an access to "experience"—unlimited amounts of it—without an actual intrusion into the passion and intimacy of others. As a creative writer, he need only infer or imagine these things to "possess" them. It is, in a certain sense, a shortcut to one's experience, and it allows an author without a deep personal acquaintance with passion and intimacy an "honest" stance in which not only to write with conviction about them but to build entire novels around them. It also may imply, as the defect of its qualities, a created representation of life that is oppressively cerebral, fastidious, and perhaps bloodless, a representation that either reconstructs human passion and intimacy through the prism of memory and imagination or does without them altogether.

With such a general framework in mind, the fact that during Isabel's midnight vigil "all goes on without her being approached by another person and without her leaving her chair" assumes added significance. It is one of the most intensive experiences in the novel, and it all takes place in an armchair, a triumph—for the novelist—of the imagination serving as the locus of experience, the imagination replacing the more conventional scenario of "caravan" and "pirate." It becomes clear that one cannot understand Isabel's European adventure without exploring the drama of her "ridiculously active" imagination. Once this drama is interpreted, Isabel's cryptic return to Rome can be seen as the inevitable conclusion to her experience abroad.

Isabel's triumphant entry into Gardencourt strikes just the exalted note James later described in his 1908 Preface. Appearing unattached, uncompromised, and as if from nowhere, with confident self-possession and energetic charm, she thoroughly enchants the Touchetts and Lord Warburton. It is Isabel's scene altogether—the winning over of the barking terrier, the assimilation of the beauties of Gardencourt ("I've been all over the house; it's too enchanting"[I,18]), her immediate and unchallenged assumption of equality ("while she lingered so near the threshold, slim and charming, her interlocutor [Ralph] wondered if she expected the old man to come and pay her his respects"[I,19]), and, underlying it all, her assertion of independence. As she enters Gardencourt, to use the phrase that recurs through the novel, the world seems to be before her, obedient to her will, decked out in the hue of her imagination: "Oh, I hoped there would be a lord; it's just like a novel!"(I,18).

Despite this triumph of her high spirits, the reader may notice that Isabel is at times surprised by the tone and manners of her company. She blushes on three occasions in this early scene: at Ralph's unexpected gift of the terrier, at Mr. Touchett's compliment to her beauty, and again at Ralph's playful remark that Mrs. Touchett has "adopted" her. Though these are minor awkwardnesses within her larger "success," yet they reverberate. This is not the only unexpected gift from Ralph that will surprise Isabel; nor will she avoid discomfort in the future when her beauty is mentioned. As to being "adopted" by Mrs. Touchett, her single-minded concern with independence keeps her from hearing the playfulness in Ralph's use of the word. This emphasis on her own independence— "I'm very fond of my liberty"(I,24)—begins to mesh in the reader's mind with a whole series of remarks made in the first chapter, and the result is strange. While her forceful personality is engaged in assimilating Gardencourt into her own manner— which is what her triumphant entry means—indeed, while in the very act of proclaiming her independence, she is at the same time being assimilated *by* Gardencourt, becoming unwittingly associated with an intricate network of verbal patterns established at Gardencourt in the first chapter. As some of those verbal patterns are examined, they begin to reveal something quite different from her spirited and romantic effusions. For, charming though that opening scene is, it has an undertone redolent of fatigue and various kinds of failure.

There we see two invalids, one dying, the other soon to die. Although Mr. Touchett's life has been successful, the narrator curiously defines that success in terms of the more appealing "inoffensiveness of failure,"(I,4), as if to assure us that Mr. Touchett has inflicted no injuries, is not obnoxious or self-assertive, as most "successful" men apparently are. His son Ralph exhibits even more of "the inoffensiveness of failure"; though young, charming, and insouciant, his health has entirely failed. As for Lord Warburton, his "illness" is psychological: a failure of interest in his own life. " 'He's sick of life,' " Ralph says, and the appropriate remedy is to " 'take hold of a pretty woman . . . He's trying hard to fall in love,' [Ralph] added, by way of explanation, to his father"(I,8,11). In this casual and urbane opening scene, the relaxed tradition of afternoon tea and the civilized habit of playful and ironic discourse blend extensively with a radical failure in the health of two men and in the interest of the third. In both respects, it would seem, nothing could be farther from the straightforward vivacity of Isabel Archer in chapter two. Yet Lord Warburton is virtually waiting for her to enter onto the scene from the wings.

In addition, "independence," that note Isabel is so often and eagerly to sound, has become, in chapter one, indelibly associated with Mrs. Touchett and her unsuccessful marriage. "Independence" explains Mr. Touchett's ignorance of where his wife is and when she will arrive, and under this ambivalent heading (present even in Mrs. Touchett's telegram) the two women are so linked that when the unannounced Isabel first appears, Lord Warburton can only identify her as "Mrs. Touchett's niece—the independent young lady"(I,17). The effect of these multiple parallels is subtly to *frame* and implicate beyond her own knowledge the impression Isabel makes in chapter two, to suggest the underside of independence, and, by inference, to qualify health by sickness, aspiration by failure, naïve eagerness by a kind of playful boredom, a potential marriage (Lord Warburton and Isabel) by a failed one (Mr. and Mrs. Touchett). These darker motifs in the first chapter complicate one's response to the second. They challenge Isabel's assertion of independence and frame the canvas on which she will move.

After Isabel's idealism and some of the elements that will "educate" that idealism have been adumbrated, James focuses on her past. Like Rowland Mallett's entrance into Roderick Hudson's life, Mrs. Touchett's appearance, virtually in the guise of a fairy godmother, has awakened in Isabel "a desire to leave the past behind her and, as she said to herself, to begin afresh"(I,41). Among other things, this repudiated "past" consists of Caspar Goodwood, whose visit she is awaiting when Mrs. Touchett arrives, and who, like fate, hovers in her vicinity throughout the novel, finally to close in for that crucial, no longer postponable confrontation in the last pages.

At the present moment, however, Isabel feels nothing but independence. "Her imagination was by habit ridiculously active; when the door was not open it jumped out of the window. She was not accustomed indeed to keep it behind bolts; and at important moments . . . she paid the penalty of having given undue encouragement to the faculty of seeing without judging"(I,42). The figure suggests freedom; Isabel's imagination impatiently rejects restrictions and insists on its own independence at the risk of being occasionally convicted of error. Even so, Isabel "had an unquenchable desire to think well of herself"(I,68). She abhors cultivating doubt of herself or of others, for with "a certain nobleness of imagination which rendered her a good many services and played her a great many tricks . . . she had a fixed determination to regard the world as a place of brightness, of free expansion, of irresistible action"(I,68). Accompanying this "nobleness of imagination" is "an infinite hope that she should never do anything wrong"(I,68). Her discovery of errors of feeling is rendered, significantly, in the figure of "a trap which might have caught her and smothered her"(I,68), and "inflicting a sensible injury upon another person . . . always struck her as the worst thing that could happen to her"(I,68). Falseness and cruelty seem to her inexcusable; on the threshold of life, she envisages perfect harmony between her appearance and inner self: "she would be what she appeared, and she would appear what she was"(I,69).

Isabel's imagination, in these passages, is virtually synonymous with her idealism; chronically given free rein, it encourages a large, romantic way of looking at life wherein character and conduct may be spotless and even heroic. Such an imagination carries its own landscape, of which the keynote is spaciousness and the appropriate symbol a garden: "Her nature had, in her conceit, a certain garden-like quality, a suggestion of perfume and murmuring boughs, of shady bowers and lengthening vistas, which made her feel that introspection was, after all, an exercise in the open air"(I,72). Through the transforming agency of the fairy godmother, Mrs. Touchett, this imagined landscape materializes, becomes Gardencourt, and romance becomes real: "Oh, I hoped there would be a lord; it's just like a novel!"

The expansiveness and independence present in Isabel's view of herself and in her scope of action contrast with the formidable limiting prerequisites imposed by that view. Before it can be realized, many conditions must be met. "Irresistible action" is desired, but always in a field devoid of cruelty, falseness, self-doubt, or injury to others—in a word, evil. Her high-flying imagination is at once superior to these inhibiting factors and yet unequipped to recognize their presence in the inevitably mixed motives at work in human affairs, at work, even, in her own affairs: "Of course the danger of a high spirit was the danger of inconsistency—the danger of keeping up the flag after the place has surrendered"(I,69).

Consequently, her projected experience is suffused with the light of perfect self-confidence and confidence in others, a light cast by her "ridiculously active" imagination, and Isabel eagerly seeks contact with the world. Certain that she is equal to its challenges, assured of the integrity of her garden-like mind, she hopes to "find herself some day in a difficult position, so that she should have the pleasure of being as heroic as the occasion demanded"(I,69). Anticipating life to correspond with what she has read of it, she feels deprived of a knowledge of the unpleasant, "for she had gathered from her acquaintance with literature that it was often a source of interest and even of instruction"(I,42). Secure within the landscape of her imagination, Isabel sets out to assimilate within that garden a lifetime of experience: "her deepest enjoyment was to feel the continuity between the movements of her own soul and the agitations of the world"(I,45).

Of course the significant experience of the world, as well as its major agitations, is to be found in Europe. There, through the media of art, social institutions, and civilized manners, the inchoate experience of mankind has been redeemed through form, made articulate and accessible in the guise of, among other things, art objects and artful human beings. The image of formed life Europe offers is compelling to Isabel because, unlike anything else she has ever known and consonant with the highest flights of her imagination, it stands so vivid and picturesque before her. It is the spectacle of "life at the remove of form and meaning; not life lived but life framed and identified."[6] Life as she anticipates it in Europe will, in its aesthetic

6. R. P. Blackmur, "A Critic's Job of Work," in *Form and Value in Modern Poetry* (Garden City, N.Y.: Doubleday, 1957), p. 339. Blackmur is speaking of the difference between poetry and life, and his words apply so closely to Isabel as to suggest that in seeking life she really wants a kind of formal beauty in her experience that only art can satisfy.

and unaggressive appeal as a spectacle, make no compromising demands upon her; it whets her appetite for experience because it does not offend the severe moral conditions of her imagination, and, thus, it answers her uneasy "mixture of curiosity and fastidiousness, of vivacity and indifference"(I,69). I say "uneasy" because, although she ardently desires "experience," she seeks it only in the ideal guise projected by her fastidious imagination.

She is unaware of the fastidiousness underlying her curiosity, however, and when she rejects Lord Warburton's proposal—her first experience of magnitude—she attributes to her desire for deeper experience a rejection that may more accurately be traced to the hypercritical demands of her imagination: "She couldn't marry Lord Warburton; the idea failed to support any enlightened prejudice in favour of the free exploration of life that she had hitherto entertained"(I,155). Territorial, political, and social are the characteristics of the system, the trap into which he would draw her, and this simply fails to appeal to her imagination, as "hitherto her visions of a completed consciousness had concerned themselves largely with moral images—things as to which the question would be whether they pleased her sublime soul"(I,143).

This rejection represents the first crucial step in Isabel's experiment, her attempt to explore life without sacrificing the requirements of her imagination, and its essentially *negative* character frightens her: "Who was she, what was she, that she should hold herself superior? What view of life, what design upon fate, what conception of happiness, had she that pretended to be larger than these large, these fabulous occasions? If she wouldn't do such a thing as that then she must do great things, she must do something greater"(I,156). What these greater things will be Isabel does not know, but she senses that to marry him would be to escape her "fate," her ultimate, if hazily envisaged, encounter with life itself.

Her immediate options (like marriage to Lord Warburton

or Caspar Goodwood) inevitably fall short of the imagined mark, and the reader may wonder if Isabel is not holding out for that form of experience which corresponds to the romantic visions of her "sublime soul," a form of experience so vaguely imagined as to be beyond what life can ever specifically offer. Such an urgent quest for life may in fact imply an even more urgent though unconscious need to reject life on any but its ideal, impossible terms.

The whole question, of course—the extent to which certain unacknowledged fears influence Isabel's behavior—is much debated among the critics. Richard Poirier offers cogent reasons for rejecting the inquiry altogether; invoking James's repeated (and untypical) pleas not to judge Isabel conventionally or uncharitably (see, especially, *Portrait*, I,69,144–145), Poirier argues that "we cannot, without changing the rhythm and the direction of the novel, decide that her general love of liberty is really a fear of the realities of particular experience." In other words, we are asked to respect the complexity and probity of her motives, to share in James's "reluctance to go beyond the public surface of those [characters] he admires."[7] However, Poirier concludes, in *The Bostonians* and later novels James did create characters—like Olive Chancellor—whose idealistic values are "explainable" as symptoms of a deep and occasionally morbid psychological need.

Although Poirier's argument is cogent, the distinction he draws between Isabel and Olive Chancellor should be partial, not complete. For in various ways the novel *is* asking us to "place" Isabel, even as, through its plot, it enriches and further refines its "portrait" of her. Yet, as Poirier cautions, the reader must summon his own most civilized resources of nuance and generosity to avoid a simplistic consistency as he engages in the act of criticizing her, just as James did in the act of creating

7. Richard Poirier, *The Comic Sense of Henry James: A Study of the Early Novels* (New York: Oxford University Press, 1960), pp. 207, 250.

her. Consequently, perceptive as they are, David Galloway's and Tony Tanner's critical readings of Isabel's character are perhaps a shade too emphatic about her "fear of life itself, of passion and instinct,"[8] and about her feeling "for the actual [being] as curtailed as her longing for the ideal is exaggerated."[9] Throughout this study I shall be in the company of those critics who question such things as Isabel's motives and her author's achievement without, I hope, impairing a sympathetic esteem for both.

In saying goodby to one of Lord Warburton's sisters, Isabel sees within her quiet eyes "the reflexion of everything she had rejected in rejecting Lord Warburton—the peace, the kindness, the honour, the possessions, a deep security and a great exclusion"(I,189). If marriage with Lord Warburton would have represented "a great exclusion," the "manner" of Madame Merle, on the other hand, "expressed the repose and confidence which come from a large experience. Experience, however, had not quenched her youth; it had simply made her sympathetic and supple. She was in a word a woman of strong impulses keep in admirable order. This commended itself to Isabel as an ideal combination"(I,250). Ideal because Isabel sees in Madame Merle the very accomplishment she is in search of: the seemingly effortless fusion of experience and charming form, the thing obtained without scars or apparent payment. Although "forty years old and not pretty," she has not lost her youth; "her expression charmed"(I,246). Madame Merle's seasoned graciousness first enchants Isabel in precisely the same way that Chad's savoir-faire enchants Strether—as a model of what might be or what might have been.

She appears at the eve of Mr. Touchett's death, when a great deal of money is bound to change hands, but it is not

8. David Galloway, *Henry James: The Portrait of a Lady* (London: Edwin Arnold, 1967), p. 47.

9. Tony Tanner, "The Fearful Self: Henry James's *The Portrait of a Lady*," *Critical Quarterly*, 7 (1965), 208.

in this possibly mercenary light that Isabel sees her. Instead, Madame Merle's opening note has the enchantment of art itself, as Isabel hears her playing the piano with skill and feeling before their actual introduction.[10] The scene perfectly conveys the poise, aesthetic refinement, and "performing" aspect of Madame Merle's character. Without in the least separating herself from life—"she appeared to have in her experience a touchstone for everything"(I,271)—Madame Merle exhibits her varied accomplishments with such grace as to have "to Isabel's imagination a sort of greatness . . . It was as if somehow she had all society under contribution, and all the arts and graces it practiced"(I,272). In a word, if Isabel seeks the richest encounter with life, she is fortunate in her new friend, for, as Ralph phrases it, "Worldly? No, she's the great round world itself!"(I,362).[11]

Her idealizing imagination and her search for experience both appealed to, Isabel becomes increasingly fond of Madame Merle; yet she is aware that if Madame Merle "had a fault it was that she was not natural . . . her nature had been too much overlaid by custom and her angles too much rubbed away. She had become too flexible, too useful, was too ripe and final"(I,273–274). Isabel wonders, in other words, if in the assimilation of the manners of the old world—the honing and smoothing and controlling of all merely personal or prickly edges of the self—there comes a point when something precious

10. In revising the novel James delicately strengthened this initial association of artistry and Madame Merle. Instead of taking her way "toward the drawing room" (1881 text), James has Isabel go "toward the source of the harmony"(I,244), Madame Merle herself.

11. In her characteristically perceptive essay on *The Portrait of a Lady* (*The English Novel: Form and Function* [New York: Harper & Brothers, 1961], pp. 211–228), Dorothy Van Ghent further discusses the attraction Madame Merle exerts upon Isabel and draws attention to the metaphoric use of doors. However, she is concerned with the doors motif primarily as it suggests intrusion and privacy, while my study focuses more concretely on the restricted role that physical experience—passion and intimacy—plays in James's fictive world. Her comments about Madame Merle are less limited than mine to the theme of the imagination.

is not sacrificed, when in the "overlay" of custom, it is not nature itself that gets "rubbed away."

However, she does not wonder excessively, and, when she suspects that something unacknowledged occurred in the past between Ralph and Madame Merle, she does not press the issue: "With all her love of knowledge she had a natural shrinking from raising curtains and looking into unlighted corners. The love of knowledge coexisted in her mind with the finest capacity for ignorance" (I,284).

The same "mixture of curiosity and fastidiousness" appears in her response to Osmond's remarks about his own past and suggests how nearly his appeal to her is related to Madame Merle's: "This would have been rather a dry account of Mr. Osmond's career if Isabel had fully believed it; but her imagination supplied the human element which she was sure had not been wanting. His life had been mingled with other lives more than he admitted . . . For the present she abstained from provoking further revelations; to intimate that he had not told her everything . . . would in fact be uproariously vulgar" (I,382–383). Here the errors of her fastidious imagination are heavily ironic, as the reader measures the distance between her conception of the unacknowledged "human element" and the actual facts of the case. Trustingly, Isabel's imagination, finding no open door, has "jumped out of the window" and created an illusion—a more desirable, a more precious Gilbert Osmond—which only subsequent experience will remove.

She first sees Osmond, as she first saw Madame Merle, in the figure of an artful performer: "she sat there as if she had been at the play and had paid even a large sum for her place . . . They [Gilbert Osmond and Madame Merle] . . . might have been distinguished performers . . . It all had the rich readiness that would have come from rehearsal" (I,355). The irony is again heavy—she will certainly pay for this performance—but it is not all one-sided, for she thinks of him unconsciously in the language of cool analysis or of appropriation; a wealthy spectator, she will get her amusement from the performance, will enjoy what it offers her: "Her mind contained no class offering a natural place to Mr. Osmond—he was a specimen apart"(I,376). After all, as Ralph reflects, she came to Europe "to see life, and fortune was serving her to her taste; a succession of fine gentlemen going down on their knees to her would do as well as anything else"(I,395). Through Madame Merle she has encountered "the great round world itself," and through Osmond she will acquire the polished proprieties of the world, he being "not conventional," but "convention itself."

Indeed, Osmond is quick to see wherein his appeal resides: "Don't you remember my telling you that one ought to make one's life a work of art? You looked rather shocked at first; but then I told you that it was exactly what you seemed to me to be trying to do with your own"(II,15). His flawless success at molding his entire life into calculated and intelligible rhythms so fascinates Isabel, so represents what she desires, as to render her, in a chilling image, passive to his will: "he could tap her imagination with his knuckle and make it ring"(II,79). In terms of the idealizing imagination and the search for experience, Isabel's drama, so far, is thoroughly intelligible; there is an inevitability about her successive and increasingly intimate rapport with the Touchetts, then Madame Merle, and finally Gilbert Osmond.

The capacity to idealize is not the only property of the imagination, however, as James makes explicit in Isabel's meditations on her inherited fortune: "She lost herself in a maze of visions; the fine things to be done by a rich, independent, generous girl who took a large human view of occasions and obligations were sublime in the mass. Her fortune therefore became to her mind a part of her better self; it gave her importance, gave her even, to her own imagination, a certain ideal beauty. What it did for her in the imagination of others is another affair"(I,321–322).

In recognizing Isabel's characteristic vocabulary—"maze of visions," "independent," "generous," "large," "sublime," "better self," "imagination," "ideal beauty"—one sees that, within Isabel's metaphoric landscape, there is always room to wander or even lose oneself without pain or suffocation. Her imagination may be occasionally naïve, self-deluded, and blind to actuality, but it is never consciously exploitative. Yet, whenever in James the imagination of one person affects the lives of others, it becomes exploitative as it sets about to mold their lives in accord with its vision.

Nowhere is this more striking than in the central scene between Ralph and his dying father. Wishing to make Isabel "entirely independent," Ralph intends only "to put it into her power to do some of the things she wants. She wants to see the world for instance. I should like to put money in her purse"(I,260). He desires to make her rich enough "to meet the requirements of . . . [her] imagination. Isabel has a great deal of imagination"(I,261). The money will set her free. Admitting that his plan is a good deal in the interest of his own "amusement," Ralph goes on to elaborate: "I shall get just the good I said a few moments ago I wished to put into Isabel's reach—that of having met the requirements of my imagination"(I,265).

Although he seeks the well-being of Isabel, Ralph does speak the language of Iago. When Mr. Touchett points out a risk in his son's plan—the danger to Isabel of fortune hunters—Ralph responds, "I think it's appreciable, but I think it's small, and I'm prepared to take it"(I,265). The thrice-repeated "I," the facile transfer of risk from Isabel to himself, and his jaunty acceptance of such a hazard indicate the degree of self-involvement within Ralph's apparently selfless sacrifice. Reduced by his illness to being a spectator with only an aesthetic interest in life, he broods over Isabel's career as though he were sculpting it—in search of the ideal form within his unshaped materials. Accepting her at her own imaginative estimate ("She's as good as her best opportunities"[I,264]), Ralph intends to transform her romance into reality, to construct a £60,000 bridge between her limitless imagination of life and the actual facts of her future experience.

It is but one step, though a big one, from Ralph Touchett to Gilbert Osmond; they are both, like Rowland Mallet, frustrated artists whose influence upon the portrait of Isabel Archer is intimately connected with their own self-fulfillment. As William Gass points out, if "the differences between Gilbert Osmond and Ralph Touchett are vast . . . they are also thin." Nevertheless, Osmond seeks to have her reflect himself alone, while Ralph, less selfishly, is interested in realizing the possibilities within the medium (Isabel) itself. Gass goes on to speculate that "there is in Isabel herself a certain willingness to be employed, a desire to be taken up and fancied . . . She is a great subject. She will make a great portrait. She knows it."[12]

Osmond's imagination, however, is concerned with other things than Isabel's aspirations: "The desire to have something or other to show for his 'parts'—to show somehow or other—had been the dream of his youth; but as the years went on the conditions attached to any marked proof of rarity had affected him more and more as gross and detestable . . . His 'style' was what the girl had discovered with a little help; and now . . . she should publish it to the world without his having any of the trouble. She should do the thing *for* him, and he would not have waited in vain"(II,12).

What the money does for her in his imagination is distinctly egotistic: it will pay for the acquisition of suitable art objects; it will establish him firmly in the society he both despises and envies. Isabel is the key to these acquisitions, as well as an apparently rare one herself, whose value increases once he

12. William Gass, "The High Brutality of Good Intentions," *Accent*, 18 (1958), 69, 68.

learns she has rejected Lord Warburton: "he perceived a new attraction in the idea of taking to himself a young lady who had qualified herself to figure in his collection of choice objects by declining so noble a hand"(II,9). The life-denying aspect of Osmond's acquisitive aestheticism is conveyed by Isabel's value deriving less from what she does or is than from the enviable Lord Warburton's inability to possess her: the value is asserted through the negative gesture, as is likewise true with Mrs. Osmond's Thursdays, "which her husband still held for the sake not so much of inviting people as of not inviting them"(II,292).

Being Osmond's "style-bearer" is heavy going for Isabel, and it is a tribute to James's craft that her appearances after her marriage, first seen from the point of view of Ned Rosier, express the extent of this change. Her "quick eagerness" is gone, she has "more the air of being able to wait"; she strikes him, indeed, as "the picture of a gracious lady"(II,105). In R. P. Blackmur's incisive words, "we have seen a bright-brash, conceited young girl whose chief attractive power lay in her money, change into a young woman who is luminous rather than bright, human rather than brash . . ."[13] Her vaunted independence and expansiveness are replaced by cautious dickering with Rosier and "covert observation"(II,178) of her husband. Osmond has impressed his forms upon her indeed, and Ralph sees that "her light step drew a mass of drapery behind it; her intelligent head sustained a majesty of ornament. The free, keen girl had become quite another person; what he saw was the fine lady who was supposed to represent something"(II,143). And what she represents, in her early talks with Rosier, her weekly Thursdays, and her painful counsels with Pansy, is, of course, Osmond.

If Osmond's imaginative design, in regard to Isabel, is almost

13. R. P. Blackmur, "Introduction to *The Portrait of a Lady,*" in *Perspectives on James's The Portrait of a Lady,* ed. William T. Stafford (New York: New York University Press, 1967), pp. 247–255.

purely exploitative, Madame Merle's is much more complex. Pansy's envisaged marriage will partly redeem her own frustrated, unsuccessful life, and Isabel's money is a crucial step in the realization of this goal.[14] With the appearance of Lord Warburton as Pansy's suitor, her design is on the verge of completion; his abrupt and unexplained departure is more than Madame Merle's patience can bear. It brings down "a palace of thought," to use James's evocative phrase from *The Sacred Fount*. There, the phrase describes the ostensible collapse, before reality, of the narrator's all-consuming imaginative vision (a collapse that reverberates throughout James's fiction). Here, it indicates the foundering of Madame Merle's carefully nurtured vision and precipitates a brutal encounter with Isabel:

"It isn't information I want. At bottom it's sympathy. I had set my heart on that marriage; the idea did what so few things do—it satisfied the imagination."

"Your imagination, yes. But not that of the persons concerned."

"You mean by that of course that I'm not concerned. Of course not directly. But when one's such an old friend one can't help having something at stake. You forget how long I've known Pansy. You mean, of course," Madame Merle added, "that *you* are one of the persons concerned."

"No; that's the last thing I mean. I'm very weary of it all."

Madame Merle hesitated a little. "Ah yes, your work's done" [II,324].

Your imagination, yes. But not that of the persons concerned. Isabel unintentionally exposes just what is exploitative and egotistical in the activity of the imagination: it always imposes

14. If she uses Isabel for the sake of Pansy, she does so, in addition, because of her chastened but unextinguished infatuation with Osmond. The best gloss for this feeling is proffered by Fanny Assingham in *The Golden Bowl:* "It would have been seen, it would have been heard of before, the case of the woman a man doesn't want, or of whom he's tired, or for whom he has no use but *such* uses, and who's capable, in her infatuation, in her passion, of promoting his interests with other women rather than lose sight of him, lose touch of him, cease to have to do with him at all" (Henry James, *The Golden Bowl* [New York: Scribner's, 1909],II,127–128).

upon "that of the persons concerned." A conflict between imaginative designs—between hers and Ralph's—is indeed what explains Isabel's own uneasiness at having inherited a fortune and the ill-fated need she feels to get rid of that fortune. Such a conflict, furthermore, underlies her more obvious discomfort under the weighty and burdensome forms required by Gilbert Osmond's imagination. The scene bristles with alternately poignant and chilling nonrecognitions. Sympathy is what Madame Merle wants, but here again she is doomed to frustration, as she can permit neither Isabel nor Pansy to learn the "legitimate" motive behind her plan—that is, her interest in her own child. The sympathy available to a mother is denied to a mere meddling friend. Isabel's rejoinder, then— "Your imagination, yes. But not that of the persons concerned"—is incisive in the truth it unconsciously expresses. Not only does she put her finger on Madame Merle's unjustifiable role in her marriage to Osmond, but she also touches—again unconsciously—on Madame Merle's hidden though profoundly justified concern with Pansy; yet Isabel touches on this only to throw into the older woman's teeth again, all unawares, the illegitimacy of her role, the isolation and helplessness to which she is condemned.[15]

In her subsequent phrase, "You forget how long I've known Pansy," the gap in experience and knowledge between Madame Merle and Isabel is conveyed, but Madame Merle's following claim that Isabel has prevented Pansy's marriage reveals an even greater gap between the two women. It is a gap between their two kinds of imagination. With her touchstone for everything, with her assumption of cool certainty, her thrice-reiterated "of course" and her facile "you mean by that" and "you forget how long" expressions, Madame Merle has yet failed

15. Nowhere is the misery of Madame Merle's false role more to be inferred than when she has to take, at Mrs. Touchett's hands, supercilious and scornful remarks about Osmond's "probably quite cold-blooded love-affairs" and about his "more or less pert little daughter . . . she's an insipid little chit" (I,398).

to place Isabel. She is unequipped, through the spots of commonness in her imagination, to assess the idealism of Isabel's imagination. Ever since Isabel's inheritance, at the announcement of which Madame Merle had blurted out, "Ah, the clever creature!"(I,298), the failure of the older woman's imagination has been discernible. In the present scene it involves the suspicion that Isabel, jealous of Pansy, wants to retain Lord Warburton for herself and has thus discouraged the match: "Ah yes, your work's done."

This failure of Madame Merle's imagination reveals to Isabel the immense failure of her own. The older woman, who "in twenty ways" presented herself to Isabel as a model, now reveals, beneath her aesthetic composure, an unsightly desire: "Let him [Lord Warburton] off—let us have him!"(II,326). Echoing Isabel's recognition of the same lie in Osmond's posture of aesthetic detachment ("How much you must want to make sure of him [Lord Warburton]!"[II,264]), Madame Merle's revealed design goads Isabel's tormented imagination into a realm as yet shunned by her, the imagination of evil. Fastidiously avoiding the role of ego and hypocrisy in human conduct, her imagination had projected an expansive life of high ideals, pure character, and heroic action. But in that scene by the dying fire—the one James so admired—she begins to acknowledge the blight that has befallen her landscape and her freedom: "She had taken all the first steps in the purest confidence, and then she had suddenly found the infinite vista of a multiplied life to be a dark, narrow alley with a dead wall at the end"(II,189).

She comes to realize that she has misjudged Osmond by indicating to him that she valued him according to his imagined conception of himself, just as, indeed, Ralph misjudged her by taking her at her own illusory estimate. And, in an exact parallel, all the money that Ralph gave her (that they might both meet the requirements of their imagination) she has given to Osmond (that *they* might both meet the requirements of their imagination). For this idealized image of himself, Osmond had admired her, and "she was to think of him as he thought of himself—as the first gentleman in Europe"(II,196–197). She now sees how deeply her imagination has played her false: "during those months she had imagined a world of things that had no substance. She had had a more wondrous vision of him, fed through charmed senses and oh such a stirred fancy!—she had not read him right"(II,192).[16]

Upon this follow still more somber insights into the ambiguous motives which her imagination shaped and which resulted in her disastrous marriage:

At bottom her money had been a burden, had been on her mind, which was filled with the desire to transfer the weight of it to some other conscience, to some more prepared receptacle. What would lighten her own conscience more effectually than to make it over to the man with the best taste in the world? Unless she should have given it to a hospital there would have been nothing better she could do with it; and there was no charitable institution in which she had been as much interested as in Gilbert Osmond. He would use her fortune in a way that would make her think better of it and rub off a certain grossness attaching to the good luck of an unexpected inheritance . . . Isabel's cheek burned when she asked herself if she had really married on a factitious theory, in order to do something finely appreciable with her money [II,193].

If in an earlier passage Isabel was described as bearing the burden of Osmond's weighty forms, here she sees herself as shifting her burden to him. And yet not to a unique human being, intrinsically valued, named Gilbert Osmond, but to "some other conscience, to some more prepared receptacle," almost to some rather superior "charitable institution." The

16. In revising the novel James went to some length to stress the deceptive nature of Isabel's imagination. For this last sentence quoted, James had originally written merely, "she had a vision of him." The "world of things" in her head is no longer assessed as potential or realizable, but is seen as without "substance"; visions are acknowledged to have been fantasies; vistas have led to dark alleys.

passage closely echoes a passage about Rowland Mallet that I examined in the first chapter, and together they indicate what is disturbing in the otherwise admirable relationships these two characters engage in: "I want to care for something or for somebody. And I want to care, don't you see? with a certain intensity; even, if you can believe it, with a certain passion. I can't just now be intense and passionate about a hospital or a dormitory" (*Roderick Hudson*, 7–8). It is this too easy transference from passion for an "institution" to passion for an individual that suggests something fundamentally depersonalized about the passion itself: the subjective imaginative energies of Rowland and Isabel, demanding an outlet, are given free rein, while the unique qualities of the other person— Roderick or Gilbert Osmond—are hardly understood at all. Thus Gilbert Osmond, once categorized, has meshed only too snugly into her imaginative web; in this sense, from the first and regardless of *his* duplicity, they have been on a false footing.

Isabel goes on, however, to "answer quickly enough that this was only half the story. It was because a certain ardour took possession of her—a sense of the earnestness of his affection and a delight in his personal qualities. He was better than anyone else . . . The finest—in the sense of being the subtlest—manly organism she had ever known had become her property, and the recognition of her having but to put out her hands and take it had been originally a sort of act of devotion" (II,193–194). This is offered, somewhat curiously, as the redeeming aspect of her feeling for Osmond; Isabel seems not to recognize the disturbing fusion of the language of affection with images of appropriation. Although she is partly giving her fortune away, she is also making sure that she gets her money's worth.

Soon, however, Osmond begins to reveal himself; and, as we saw earlier with Madame Merle, the pettiness of his imagination emerges most clearly when he attributes a similar pettiness to Isabel. As he attacks her for preventing Pansy's marriage to Lord Warburton, "it came over her, after he had said this, that she had once thought him beautiful"(II,264). Realizing now that his interest in her is purely as an emblem of his own style, and that the style itself—the traditions it symbolizes—is "hideously unclean"(II,200), Isabel recoils, resists: "She had pleaded the cause of freedom, of doing as they chose, of not caring for the aspect and denomination of their life—the cause of other instincts and longing, of quite another ideal"(II,199). The Europe he represents, she comes finally to see, is in its petty rapacity and rigid formalism a mockery of her envisaged synthesis of experience and the idealizing imagination, of "the union of great knowledge with great liberty"(II,198). Great liberty is just what Gilbert Osmond cannot allow: "The real offence, as she ultimately perceived, was her having a mind of her own at all"(II,200).

With her growing recognition of the exploitative and injurious effects of the imagination—hers and others'—Isabel's ideal of the union of experience and form begins to crumble. Experience, as Roderick Hudson discovered, is an undermining, corruptive agent; formal charm, as with Osmond and Madame Merle, conceals rather than redeems the corruption. The metaphors of art take on in retrospect the meaning of surface artifice, while aesthetic detachment is seen as a mask for covetous and exploitative egotism. Madame Merle's fusion of experience and unimpeachable charm is only apparent; it is not that she has no faults, but, as Mrs. Touchett with unintentional irony declares to Isabel, "You won't discover a fault in her"(I,277). Immersed as a heroine within her own romance, Isabel had envisaged a life raised to the level of art. But the romance has turned sour; "they were strangely married, at all events, and it was a horrible life"(II,202).

Before discussing the conclusion of Isabel's experiment in living, her return to Rome, and the implications of that conclusion, we might reflect on some of the gathering meanings of imagination in the novel as they affect Isabel's experience. Between the idealizing imagination of Isabel (and, subordinately, of Ralph Touchett) and the exploitative, "grasping imagination" of Madame Merle and of Gilbert Osmond, there is a serious distinction. But it is not an absolute one, and it would be as misleading to ignore the idealistic element of Madame Merle's design for Pansy as it would be to deny the unconsciously exploitative aspect of Ralph's and Isabel's nobler intentions.

Subsuming both these views of the imagination and implicit in each is the artistic imagination—both manipulative and liberating, exploitative and protective—the creative agency within himself that James so profoundly and critically explored in his fiction. The *human* implications of the artistic impulse are of course massive. In this connection the relations between James, the characters in his novels, and his readers have been brilliantly explored by Laurence Holland, who suggests that "James's art does not define the hazards of a philosophical position so much as perfect a form of tact in dealing with the personal and social relations which inhere at once in the conduct of an author's characters, in his conduct with them, and in his behavior with his reader."[17]

At this point it is sufficient to add that in the act of imagining a character, James saw "an act of personal possession of one being by another,"[18] that in the process of imagining an "ado" for Isabel, he created the plot which betrayed her freedom and idealism, that the impulse for definitive form has in it the seeds of both idealism and exploitation, that to be entertained by art means to be "living at the expense of someone else,"[19] and that, for James, to write novels means, in a general

17. Laurence B. Holland, *The Expense of Vision: Essays on the Craft of Henry James* (Princeton, N.J.: Princeton University Press, 1964), p. 224. I am deeply indebted to this work.

18. James, *Art of the Novel*, p. 37.

19. Henry James, *Partial Portraits* (London, 1888), pp. 227–228, quoted in Holland, *Expense of Vision*, p. 127.

way, to be a perpetual eavesdropper and to get one's experience vicariously.

In other words, the creative act in literature implies for the novelist a multifaceted form of behavior toward two worlds: the one he lives in and the one he begets. And James is acutely aware that his own activity inescapably shares one of those traits that his work so comprehensively and critically analyzes: the exploitation of one human being by another.

The language of exploitation, consequently, is varied and omnipresent in James's fiction. It is particularly noticeable in his description of artist-figures; and, thinking of Osmond and Madame Merle, Isabel recognizes "that she had been an applied handled hung-up tool, as senseless and convenient as mere shaped wood and iron"(II,379). A more extreme illustration from *Roderick Hudson,* chilling in its sexual undertone, occurs in Gloriani's comment about Roderick's use of Christina as a model: "but you oughtn't to have let her off with the mere sacrifice of her head. There would be no end to be done with the whole inimitable presence of her. If I could only have got hold of her I would have pumped every inch of her empty"(189). About this much might be said, and I will take it up again later, along with some larger questions about the role of the artist-figure in James's work, in my discussion of *The Sacred Fount.*

Most pertinent now is the conflict between idealism and exploitation and the crisis its discovery brings to Isabel: is spacious self-development, unrestricted personal independence, according to the requirements of the imagination, morally consonant with her painful experience of the great world? Or does self-development necessarily imply exploitation of others? Her uncompromising preference for Osmond, inevitably giving pain to Ralph and his mother, brings home to Isabel a somber realization: "It was the tragic part of happiness; one's right was always made of the wrong of some one else"(II,78).

If this is so, the world is a very small place indeed; to take a deep, self-developing breath is, morally speaking, to cause those nearby almost to suffocate. In thinking, just prior to her marriage, that "the world lay before her—she could do whatever she chose"(II,36), Isabel could not have been more mistaken, and Osmond's philosophy of silent and dignified resignation, while hypocritical, contains a precious truth: "I don't mean to say I've cared for nothing; but the things I've cared for have been definite—limited"(I,382). Something like Osmond's silence is present in her refusal to "publish" her mistake, and something like his acceptance of fixed limits underlies her belief that "when a woman had made such a mistake, there was only one way to repair it—just immensely (oh, with the highest grandeur!) to accept it. One folly was enough, especially when it was to last forever; a second one would not much set it off"(II,161).

Here, finally, the ideal of expansive self-development makes its peace with the newly discovered law of limits. Action itself, the plane of "things being done," is tempting but doomed: the single thing that can succeed one folly is another. Honor resides, as so often in James, in the refusal to escape from a bad situation; self-development is possible only in terms of the "sublime soul."[20] The tone of the passage just quoted is latent with this meaning, as the somber acceptance of life's limits is relieved only by the welling up of idealistic fervor in the parenthetic phrase. In revising the earlier version of this passage James stressed the distinction between physical helplessness and spiritual fulfillment by adding the words, "just immensely (oh, with the highest grandeur!)." The passage

20. It is interesting to interpret James's use of "sublime" in the scientific sense of "sublimation," the passage from solid to spirit. In addition, the psychological meaning of "sublimation," with its morbid overtones, seems to me relevant in describing the attitude toward the body that James's fiction conveys. These more than human physical renunciations are precisely what is later implied by Madame de Vionnet's poignant and bitter confession to Strether: "And I who should have liked to seem to you—well, sublime!" (*The Ambassadors* [New York: Scribner's, 1909],II,288.)

would be rather bleak without them. Even with them, though, the inability of the feeling essentially to alter the action is conveyed by the inability of the parenthesis to alter the basic grammatical structure of the sentence. In short, Isabel's idealism is incapable of influencing her further experience at the level of positive action, is only parenthetically fused with it. If independence and expansiveness are not consonant with the facts of experience, they are nevertheless too valuable to relinquish, and they retire to the realms of spirit and imagination, realms that take up no room at all.

What, finally, are the components of Isabel's experience? Sporadically throughout the novel the two "unconverted" Americans, Caspar Goodwood and Henrietta Stackpole, proclaim how unrecognizably changed Isabel is by the impact of Europe. But "Europe" is an immense and amorphous agent of change, and, with the exception of her response to Rome, the novel focuses very little upon Isabel's reaction to Europe itself. Her experience comes, instead, largely from her encounter with representative Europeans abroad, be they British or "Europeanized" Americans. This roughly means, apart from Goodwood and Madame Merle, the men she meets as suitors or potential suitors, for, according to Ralph, "She had wanted to see life, and fortune was serving her to her taste; a succession of fine gentlemen going down on their knees to her would do as well as anything else" (I, 395).

If the proposals constitute one of her chief experiences abroad, *The Portrait* is very much a novel revolving around a central love concern. But James's intention in the Preface to let her, unconventionally, create her own fate is likewise borne out, for the major interest in the proposals resides in Isabel's refusal of them. " 'Place the center of the subject in the young woman's own consciousness,' I [James] said to myself, 'and you get as interesting and as beautiful a difficulty as you could wish. Stick to *that*—for the centre; put the heaviest weight into *that* scale, which will be so largely the scale of her relation to herself . . . press least hard, in short, on the consciousness of your heroine's satellites, especially the male; make it an interest contributive only to the greater one.' "[21]

At this point an interesting connection appears between James's emphasis through technique on Isabel's interior life (an emphasis that this chapter began by observing) and the curiously fastidious nature of Isabel's experience itself. For, in focusing relentlessly on Isabel's interior drama, James does precisely what his heroine does; he gives short shrift to the impinging males. They impede the desired development. Thinking too much about marriage is vulgar, and Isabel "held that a woman ought to be able to live to herself, in the absence of exceptional flimsiness, and that it was perfectly possible to be happy without the society of a more or less coarse-minded person of another sex"(I,71). This rather disturbing point of view and the combination of fastidiousness and independence, joined with the belief that under certain ideal conditions "she could give herself completely"(I,72), make a brief study of the proposals pertinent to our analysis of Isabel's imagination and experience.

When Lord Warburton comes to make his offer, Isabel guesses his intention and wishes both to "elude" it and "to satisfy her curiosity about it"(I,142). The offer itself, as an offer, interests her, but *what* is offered is repugnant to her fastidiousness, is "an aggression almost to the degree of an affront"(I,143). Yet, as Ralph saw, it does constitute an experience and, as such, it contributes to Isabel's development, to her "portrait." Lord Warburton, in the compromise represented by his reiterated proposals, soon becomes for Isabel, "Poor Lord Warburton!" He becomes ludicrous and miserable, but Isabel remains firm: "You may be unhappy, but you shall

---

21. James, *Art of the Novel,* p. 51.

not make *me* so. That I can't allow"(I,421). When he appears in Rome, prior to the marriage, he is indeed "Poor Lord Warburton," and Isabel soon sends him packing back to London, unsparingly reduced to "pitifully" whining and blushing "like a boy of fifteen"(II,7). And, when Lord Warburton later reappears in her life, there is still an element of cruelty in her reflection that "there was something in his friendship that appeared a kind of resource in case of indefinite need; it was like having a large balance at the bank"(II,212).

In this vein one may find equally disturbing Isabel's gratuitous remark to Edward Rosier—why, after all, should she tell him "that, old friends as we are, if you had done me the honour to ask me to marry you I should have refused you on the spot"(II,208)? Further, when she learns from Ralph that the dying Mr. Touchett is a great admirer of hers, Isabel's first reaction is not tenderness or pity but "a small sigh of relief" that he was at least one "who couldn't propose to marry her"(I,238). Finally, when Ralph confesses that his love for her has prompted his criticism of Osmond, we read that "Isabel turned pale: was he too on that tiresome list? She had a sudden wish to strike him off"(II,21–22). Without carping, one may detect in the vindictive, shrill, and self-defensive tenor of these feelings of Isabel a mildly obsessive need to ward off or even humiliate her male admirers; such feelings, needless to say, complicate our sense of her otherwise "free exploration of life."

If Isabel's relationship with her "European" suitors contains this uneasy, antagonistic element, her attitude toward Caspar Goodwood verges upon outright hostility:

For however she might have resisted conquest at her English suitor's large quiet hands she was at least as far removed from the disposition to let the young man from Boston take positive possession of her . . . for it was part of the influence he had upon her that he seemed to deprive her of the sense of freedom. There was a disagreeably strong push, a kind of hardness of presence, in his way of rising before her . . . She might like it or

not, but he insisted, ever, with his whole weight and force . . .
The idea of a diminished liberty was particularly disagreeable
to her at present, since she had just given a sort of personal
accent to her independence by looking so straight at Lord Warburton's big bribe and yet turning away from it[I,161–162].

One needn't be sexually preoccupied to perceive the sexual
tenor of this passage: Isabel thinks in terms of "conquest" and
"positive possession." Lord Warburton's hands are rather chill-
ingly "large" and "quiet," while Goodwood's threat is unambiguously physical: "disagreeably strong push," "hardness of
presence," "rising before her," an insistence "with his whole
weight." These phrases (plus the distinctly phallic image of
the "big bribe" which Isabel looks straight at and then rejects—the phrase was added in revision to replace the less vivid
"lures") make us realize that, however much her European
experience is a quest, it is also a flight from Caspar Goodwood,
a quest and a flight that will be just as confusingly intertwined
in Isabel's final journey to Rome.

I am not suggesting that her other criticisms of Caspar Goodwood are mere rationalizations of this unacknowledged fear.
In his rigid, artless, self-defined self-acceptance, Goodwood
is the antithesis of the identity Isabel seeks to create through
her encounter with European civilization. Still, it is significant
that after rejecting Goodwood in London Isabel drops on her
knees and trembles, partly yielding "to the satisfaction of having refused two ardent suitors in a fortnight. That love of
liberty of which she had given Caspar Goodwood so bold a
sketch was as yet almost exclusively theoretic . . . But it appeared to her she had done something; she had tasted of the
delight, if not of battle, at least of victory; she had done what
was truest to her plan"(I,233). The element of morbidity in
this "plan," manifest in the satisfaction of refusing two suitors
and in the battle metaphor, beclouds her idealistic "love of
liberty" and suggests the magnitude of the role played by sexual
feelings in Isabel's grand design.

It is, consequently, interesting that the two most intimate and moving scenes in the book—Isabel's embracing of Pansy at the convent and her last words with Ralph—both make use, at their climax, of the figure of siblings, not of lovers: "Then they held each other a moment in a silent embrace, like two sisters"(II,386). "'Oh my brother!' she cried with a movement of still deeper prostration"(II,417).

In contrast, the two major scenes dealing with sexual passion both focus on Caspar Goodwood, and they are fearful and repulsive to Isabel. The first occurs in Rome, as Goodwood, frustrated, is about to depart. "Now that he was alone with her all the passion he had never stifled surged into his senses; it hummed in his eyes and made things swim round him . . . If he had seen more distinctly he would have perceived her smile was fixed and a trifle forced—that she was frightened at what she saw in his own face"(II,317).

The second encounter, the last scene in the book, is perhaps James's most unrestrained presentation of the mixed terror and appeal of sexual passion. As Goodwood pleads with Isabel to give up her independence and rely on him, she outwardly resists but realizes, only now, "that she had never been loved before. She had believed it, but this was different, this was the hot wind of the desert, at the approach of which the others dropped dead, like mere sweet airs of the garden. It wrapped her about; it lifted her off her feet, while the very taste of it, as of something potent, acrid and strange, forced open her set teeth"(II,433–434). This is the ultimate threat to Isabel's inviolate, garden-like soul. To succumb to him is to let go altogether, to sacrifice her precious sense of herself to his more aggressive and passionate identity, and, with remarkable candor, James has rendered the threat in unambiguous sexual imagery.

With unconscious irony Goodwood remonstrates, "It's too monstrous of you to think of sinking back into that misery, of going to open your mouth to that poisoned air"(II,434).

The air *is* poisoned in Rome—Osmond's distrust and egotism account for that—but it is no easier to breathe in Goodwood's presence. Contact with either man means the devastation of the garden, of ideal self-development:

He glared at her a moment through the dusk, and the next instant she felt his arms about her and his lips on her own lips. His kiss was like white lightning, a flash that spread, and spread again, and stayed; and it was extraordinarily as if, while she took it, she felt each thing in his hard manhood that had least pleased her, each aggressive fact of his face, his figure, his presence, justified of its intense identity and made one with this act of possession. So had she heard of those wrecked and under water following a train of images before they sink. But when darkness returned she was free[II,436].

Free from Caspar Goodwood, but free only to return to Gilbert Osmond ("One folly was enough, especially when it was to last forever; a second one would not much set it off"). Again, liberation is also flight.

It would be impossible to determine exactly why Isabel decides to marry Osmond, but, at the least, his air of unruffled aesthetic disinterest represents no sexual threat. In this connection one of her descriptions of him is particularly suggestive: "the finest—in the sense of being the subtlest—manly organism she had ever known had become her property, and the recognition of her having but to put out her hands and take it had been originally a sort of act of devotion"(II,194). Her love vocabulary harks back to scenes with Lord Warburton and Caspar Goodwood, and one may speculate that the sexual menace implied by Warburton's "big bribe" and more strongly by Goodwood's "way of rising before her" has here come under control; Osmond's masculinity is rendered as an unthreatening "manly organism" which she can manipulate and possess. She explains her repudiation of all "her [earlier] aspirations, her theories" by "the fact that he was her lover, her own"(II,82).

This suggests desire on her part, but it is immediately followed by "and that she should be able to be of use to him. She could surrender to him with a kind of humility, she could marry him with a kind of pride; she was not only taking, she was giving"(II,82). In her need to justify "surrender" to Osmond, one may suspect that, beneath the surface nobility of her sentiment, Isabel's former repugnance to marriage has not so much vanished as been sublimated; marriage, *if* it is ideal and permits the execution of "some private duty"(II,82)—and not otherwise—is acceptable and then worthy of pride.

Perhaps for this reason the unexciting union between Henrietta Stackpole and Bantling rather disappoints Isabel ("There was a want of originality in her marrying him—there was even a kind of stupidity"[II,400]). Certainly her own union deteriorates, and there is fine irony in the fact that Osmond marries her indeed because "she is not only taking, but giving," and that the detached, unthreatening Osmond reveals himself to be exploitative and possessive to the highest degree. Thereupon ensues the attack on her own integrity, the attempt to remove her ideas and make her accept traditions she thinks "hideously unclean"(II,200).

One perceives an essential duality in Isabel's response to this attack. At the level of positive action, of physical experience, she does nothing for herself, seems to make the necessary compromises, represents Osmond, and displays those beautiful polished forms of civilization that she so admired in Madame Merle and her husband and that are the dismay of poor, plaintalking Caspar Goodwood: "You're somehow so still, so smooth, so hard. You're completely changed. You conceal everything"(II,318). Nothing could be closer to Isabel's initial impression of Madame Merle—so smooth, so ripe, so complete—and Caspar Goodwood unwittingly describes one of the things—an artful and self-protective surface manner—that Isabel has learned from her experience. Unlike Madame Merle, however, Isabel still retains her inner integrity. Experience is corrupting but she will not allow it to corrupt her; she wears a mask but she has not been "vile."

This distinction between the two women is fundamental, and James suggests it earlier through Isabel's awareness that Madame Merle "was in a word too perfectly the social animal . . . she had rid herself of every remnant of that tonic wildness . . ."(I,274). As for Isabel herself, when Lord Warburton proposes, "though she was lost in admiration of her opportunity, she managed to move back into the deepest shade of it, even as some wild, caught creature in a vast cage" (I,152–153). That "wild, caught creature" seems to suggest the inviolate, uncompromised self, the essentially private "tonic wildness" that Madame Merle has rid herself of. The vast cage in which it is caught implies the necessarily restricted realm of action within which it can retain its integrity—the essential conflict with free exploration and experience. Paradoxically, to come out of the cage is to give up freedom; to emerge into the vast chaotic world that Caspar Goodwood offers at the end of the novel is to lose the precious sense of self-identity that thrives, in James's fiction, almost exclusively on privation. So long as, under the influence of her idealizing imagination, active experience was consonant with the retention of total integrity, so long as there was no duplicity, no cruelty, no exploitation, then Isabel could maintain her romantic belief in the fusion of unfettered self-development and profound immersion in the careers of others, the affairs of the world.

But as her experience becomes less the thing done and more the temptation resisted or the deception understood, a new form for it may be seen to evolve. The crucial thing is not that Lord Warburton proposes—though that is indispensable—but that Isabel refuses. "If she wouldn't do such things as that then she must do great things, she must do something greater." Her negations of what actuality offers are the truly formative events, Isabel's real experience, negations in the service of an imaginative ideal to which actuality is increasingly unequal. Gilbert Osmond hasn't a chance; Ralph does not exaggerate when he says, "As a fact you think nothing in the world too perfect for you"(I,210). Finally, it is the perceived inadequacy of Osmond himself, the failure of their marriage, the recognition of the blindness of her imagination that give her the measure of what was to be her greatest experience and that most definitively form her.

She will not, by trying again, commit another folly; the intimate encounters with others, with the great world, having proved radically inadequate, are not redeemable by further encounters, only by spiritual acceptance, inner superiority. To be heroic—as with Christopher Newman, Catherine Sloper, and Fleda Vetch—is to avoid the proposed action. Temptations, in James, are almost inevitably to *do* something, and in the context of his work it is almost always not worth doing. Thus Isabel is tempted, after learning from the Countess Gemini of Osmond's deceit, to "be a little easy and natural and nasty; feel a little wicked, for the comfort of it, once in your life!"(II,371). She is equally tempted to cut Madame Merle dead in that final interview: "There was a moment during which, if she had turned and spoken, she would have said something that would hiss like a lash. But she closed her eyes, and then the hideous vision dropped"(II,379). Finally she is urged, by both Henrietta Stackpole and Caspar Goodwood, to flee from Osmond. In every case the temptation is to "let go"; in every case she resists.

She returns to her husband, then, for several mixed reasons, some conscious and some unconscious. By attempting to salvage Pansy's future she can at least endow her own marriage with that much positive purpose, as well as resist cynicism toward the institution itself,[22] thus retaining her vision of it as "a mag-

22. In his final revision, James emphasized the gravity of Isabel's feeling about the moral commitment entailed by marriage. The 1881 text reads: "a woman should abide with her husband," while the revised edition reads: "a woman should cleave to the man with whom, uttering tremendous vows, she had stood at the altar"(II,361).

nificent form"(II,356) against the pressures of her own experience to see it as "that ghastly form"(II,433). She must, furthermore, accept full responsibility for her own behavior, even where that behavior was manifestly influenced by the deception of others, for only by taking it all upon herself can she continue to believe in—indeed, to create—her power to control her own destiny. To return to Osmond is, therefore, to deny that her grand experiment in living has ended unsuccessfully, or in fact has ended at all. Following the dictates of her own will in this final choice, Isabel thus preserves, if only by her isolated example, her unrelinquished ideals of free will and honor. The book ends, as it began, with a failed marriage balanced by the prospects of a future, undetermined one.

And yet, intertwined about these reasons, are other, darker ones. Where else, after all, can Isabel turn? There are no viable alternatives, and Osmond, at least, is a known quantity. Experience has been found to be greatly deceptive, resulting only in the humanizing discipline of suffering, but otherwise unequal to her fastidious, imagined conception of it; the only thing worse than one folly is a second one. James hints that "life would be her business for a long time to come"(II,392)—hers will be no simple renunciation—but one may wonder what kind of future this "scene of the rest of my life"(II,398) could lead to. If this is not a tragedy, as James seems thus to suggest, it can only be because the death of concrete self-fulfillment— the acceptance of a loveless marriage—does not seem tragic to James. If living with Osmond is not tragic, one is led to assume that that aspect of life, when it goes rotten, does not strike James as important enough to be tragic.

Whatever James's intention, the somber power of the book's conclusion outweighs the author's paragraph of more hopeful or equivocating words. Assuredly, "the *whole* of anything is never told,"[23] but at the end of *The Portrait of a Lady* we do know that Isabel Archer is a tragic figure, betrayed by

23. *The Notebooks of Henry James,* ed. F. O. Matthiessen and Kenneth B. Murdock (New York: Oxford University Press, 1947), p. 18.

her own ideals, undefeated, perhaps, but essentially and permanently untriumphant.

The imagined ideal of experience not only cannot be realized, but it also poisons possible action, as Osmond's blighting touch poisons Isabel's intended action and transforms it "to slow renunciation"(II,357). Honor and the requirements of the idealizing imagination, it seems, cannot be squared with a great deal of human activity and experience, particularly with human passion, in which, as Isabel grimly realizes, "one's right was always made of the wrong of someone else."

Fastidiousness in this sense infuses the life of *The Portrait of a Lady,* and, I would hazard, accounts for much mature dissatisfaction with James, even among readers who respond to the beauty and power of his work. One recalls that odd phrase in the first chapter about the look of the "inoffensiveness of failure" present in Mr. Touchett's face which refines, as it were, the grossness out of his successful immersion in the world. One remembers that the hero of the book, Ralph, is not only an invalid but has "a secret hoard of indifference . . . [which] came to his aid and helped to reconcile him to sacrifice, since at the best he was too ill for aught but that arduous game"(I,52).[24]

One reflects, furthermore, that in the convent Pansy "didn't presume to judge others, but she had judged herself; she had seen the reality . . . She bowed her pretty head to authority and only asked of authority to be merciful"(II,385). "Reality," the plane of active experience and intimacy with others, seems, for Pansy, to be a hopeless conflict with various authorities; neither she nor Isabel can creatively reckon with it. Pansy,

24. Analogies aren't proof, but they are interesting. Consider James's strikingly similar remarks to Grace Norton, when he was discussing *The Portrait of a Lady:* "I am unlikely ever to marry . . . One's attitude toward marriage is a fact—the most characteristic part doubtless of one's general attitude toward life . . . If I were to marry I should be guilty in my own eyes of inconsistency—I should pretend to think quite a little better of life than I really do." (F. O. Matthiessen, *Henry James: The Major Phase* [New York: Oxford University Press, 1944], p. 50.)

for her part, expects very little from "reality"; she is content to retreat within her inviolable self where all things are possible: "there was no bitterness in her heart; there was only the sweetness of fidelity to Edward Rosier, and a strange, exquisite intimation that she could prove it better by remaining single than even by marrying him" (II,257).

To be sure, Isabel's drama is less clear-cut, and yet the analogy is there. Both spur and solace, the imagination begets visions, visions which are beyond what life offers and which must be, finally, relinquished, qualified, or cherished and attained in the imagination alone. The realization and enactment of that choice constitutes one of the central dramas of James's later fiction, as we turn next to *What Maisie Knew*.

III   Resisting the Assault of Experience:
What Maisie Knew

*Successfully to resist (to resist, that is, the strain of observation
and the assault of experience) what would that be, on the part
of so young a person, but to remain fresh . . . and to have
even a freshness to communicate?—the case being with Maisie
to the end that she treats her friends to the rich little spectacle
of objects embalmed in her wonder.*

Preface to What Maisie Knew

IT IS DIFFICULT TO DESCRIBE PRECISELY what changes occur
in James's fictive world between the eighties and the nineties,
but anyone who picks up *What Maisie Knew* after *The Portrait
of a Lady* (or even *The Tragic Muse* [1889–1890]) will agree
that something radical has happened.

The contours of the external world depicted in *The Spoils
of Poynton, The Other House, What Maisie Knew, The Awkward Age,* and *The Sacred Fount* are less ample than in the
early works. Poynton and Ricks, Eastmead and Bounds, the
home of Ida or Mrs. Beale or Mrs. Brook, the country house
in *The Sacred Fount*—these remain, with fugitive excursions
into the London parks or Boulogne or Mr. Longdon's country
house (so different from Newmarch!), the essential boundaries
of the action. What experience takes place must do so either
within these confines or with reference to them, and there is
a sort of suffocating constriction in Maisie's meaningless shut-

tling from one "home" to the other, in Nanda's being confronted with either the salon world or total withdrawal, and in the portentous, inescapable, hothouse atmosphere of Newmarch.

Accompanying this diminished scene of activity is an even more reduced scope of activity: sexual innuendo, intrigue, or intimacy is virtually at the center of what is happening or conjectured to be happening, and innocence in this area constitutes a much greater exclusion than in the earlier novels. Such is the setting; such, to a large degree, are the concerns that make up the oppressive "outside" world in the novels of the nineties. If it is more odious than the world of James's previous novels and more limited in the options it offers, the corresponding alternative is a more massive retreat than we have yet witnessed into the innocence or delusion of the untutored, imaginative, and outcast mind. And this, oddly, will have a liberating effect.

If the spectrum of experience is diminished in the sense mentioned above, it becomes less limited, literally less defined, in another. If little is going on, there is virtually no consensus among the different characters about what that "little" is: the activity within the novel tends to expand hazily into a set of various possible actions rather than clarify itself as a single well-defined one. (*The Sacred Fount* represents the extreme development of this tendency.) This occurs because "what is going on" is almost wholly, in James's later work, something reflected from the mind of one or more characters; mere event or plot objectively depicted seems hardly to interest him at all.

Rather, the perceiving mind—particularly during the moments of perception—has begun to engross the author's attention to such a degree that what appeared exceptional in *The Portrait*—Isabel's sitting alone "motionlessly seeing"—is, with a few changes, the *modus operandi* of *What Maisie Knew* and *The Sacred Fount*. I say "exceptional in *The Portrait*" because Isabel, traveling from Albany to London to Paris to

Rome, meeting the Touchetts and Madame Merle, being wooed by Lord Warburton and Gilbert Osmond, seems to be a character always *doing* something, and the ramifications of what she does, the "ado" for Isabel Archer, form the sizable plot—the spectrum of experience—of that novel. But, as I have argued, the "sitting alone" scene is not really so exceptional; it represents, in fact, the most significant "activity" Isabel engages in: the imaginative, isolated exploration of her own "case." The implications of that scene were explored in the last chapter, and I suggest that *What Maisie Knew* and particularly *The Sacred Fount* are largely composed of similar scenes. Isabel's physical isolation in chapter xlii, however, is replaced by what is virtually an unbroken psychic isolation on the part of Maisie and the narrator in the *Fount*. Oppressively surrounded by others and riddled by contact with bewildering relationships on all sides, these two characters yet remain essentially alone.

Because the protagonist in these novels is separated from the activity he is attempting to understand, the reader is necessarily presented not with a crisply defined plot, but with someone's imagined (and perhaps muddled) speculations about a plot. And, in a general sense, from *What Maisie Knew* to *The Golden Bowl,* the source of the misunderstanding involves an ignorance of, or an exclusion from, sexual passion. Moreover, since James limits himself as never before to the vision of the innocent, perceiving mind, imagination becomes the faculty that the main character must develop in order to understand what the other characters are doing, and how this affects him. Given James's refusal to step in and clarify, these novels can become, it will be readily acknowledged, narrow, obsessive studies of the nature of the imagination and of its capacity for infinite speculation about those experiences of shared intimacy and passion from which it is cut off.

Opposing this liability, however, is a remarkable increase in tonal possibilities that becomes apparent in all the novels of the nineties and the next decade. By permitting the narrative voice to speak with the intimate, interior tone of his center of consciousness, James can achieve effects of poignancy hitherto impossible (tenderness, to my mind, is what is so lacking in that brilliant novel *The Bostonians*). However, James does not limit himself to the appealing effects of the subjective voice in these novels. He effortlessly moves between outer and inner perspectives, and the different kinds of vision each permits is very close to the difference between the real and romantic, as James defines these in the Preface to *The American:*

The real represents to my perception the things we cannot possibly *not* know, sooner or later, in one way or another; it being but one of the accidents of our hampered state, and one of the incidents of their quantity and number, that particular instances have not yet come our way. The romantic stands, on the other hand, for the things that, with all the facilities in the world, all the wealth and all the courage and all the wit and all the adventure, we never *can* directly know; the things that can reach us only through the beautiful circuit and subterfuge of our thought and our desire.[1]

The conflict in this passage—the obvious preference for the romantic opposed by the concomitant awareness of the real— seems to have led to the creation of a style in which both perspectives operate. Thus, James need not sacrifice the "normative," realistic perspective born of distance, and comedy can mingle unexpectedly with pathos, as in this passage from *What Maisie Knew:*

She [Mrs. Wix] had struck her at first, just after Miss Overmore, as terrible; but something in her voice at the end of an hour touched the little girl in a spot that had never even yet been reached. Maisie knew later what it was, though doubtless she couldn't have made a statement of it: these were things that a few days' talk with Mrs. Wix quite lighted up. The principal

1. Henry James, *The Art of the Novel,* ed. R. P. Blackmur (New York: Scribner's, 1934), pp. 31–32.

one was a matter Mrs. Wix herself always immediately mentioned: she had had a little girl quite of her own, and the little girl had been killed on the spot. She had had absolutely nothing else in all the world, and her affliction had broken her heart. It was comfortably established between them that Mrs. Wix's heart was broken. What Maisie felt was that she had been, with passion and anguish, a mother, and that this was something Miss Overmore was not, something (strangely, confusingly) that mamma was even less.

So it was that in the course of an extraordinarily short time she found herself as deeply absorbed in the image of the little dead Clara Matilda, who, on a crossing in the Harrow Road, had been knocked down and crushed by the cruellest of hansoms, as she had ever found herself in the family group made vivid by one of seven [Miss Overmore is one of seven sisters].[2]

The blend of pathos and comedy, as the narrator draws the reader in and out of Maisie's mind, is subtle and effective. At first the narrator is describing "from outside" Maisie's reaction to Mrs. Wix. Although these may be matters about which Maisie is incapable of making "a statement," the seriousness of her feeling is not in question. Delicately, though, the passage begins to change. "Always" cuts deftly into the increasing pathos by suggesting how frequently Mrs. Wix tells Maisie her story, while "quite of her own" expresses the child's ingenuous surprise that this old lady could also have been a mother, which brings us closer to the girl's mind. The grief of Mrs. Wix is conveyed in a limpid, unrestrained sentence, which would seem sentimental if it weren't coming from Maisie's youthful consciousness. What follows, then ("It was comfortably established . . ."), mildly jolts us out of our increasing concern by making us draw back as it articulates the lurking comic aspect of the scene: that Mrs. Wix rather enjoys her

2. *What Maisie Knew* (New York: Scribner's, 1908), pp. 23–24. Subsequent quotations from *What Maisie Knew* refer to this edition (Volume XI, 1–363, of the New York Ed.); hereafter, all page references will be included within the text, parenthetically, after the quotation.

broken heart and that Maisie innocently enjoys it too. The withdrawal, however, is only partial, or perhaps a better word would be latent. The statement still conveys the naïve consciousness of Maisie, but the tone of "comfortably established between them" has comic implications (appreciated by the narrator) that escape her and provide a larger perspective on the grief.

After this moment of gentle irony, the emotive power of the next sentence, with its fusion of adult and childlike vocabulary and syntax, is surprisingly strong. The groping rhythms in the latter part of the sentence, the naïve questioning about what a mother is, the use of the word "mamma" all locate the sentence within Maisie's mind and create the desired effect of immediacy and poignancy. Yet without the conceptual, adult perspective of "passion" and "anguish" the meaning, felt only from within, would be blurred, and the sentence would lose half its impact. In the next paragraph the narrator again effortlessly shifts back to the comic perspective—somehow still inside Maisie's mind but intent on putting the reader at a distance—with the use of the single adjective "cruellest." By remaining within the girl's mind and choosing just the proper words to bring the reader in (poignancy) or keep him out (comic detachment), James is able to achieve rich and varied effects.

Clearly, then, although the arena of physical possibilities—the realm of experience—diminishes for James's characters in these novels, there is, at the same time, a significant increase in the range and beauty of their imaginative perceptions. This increase in mental speculations and decrease of actual options can be expressed by the image of two concentric circles, one expanding as the other contracts; and Georges Poulet comments on such a dual movement of expansion and contraction in James's fiction:

The Henry James novel advances by a movement often almost imperceptible, but it never marks time, and its progression is one of an understanding that wishes to be patient and meticulous.

And in a sense, as it approaches the center, it is true to say of the investigative thought, that it turns in a narrower and narrower circle. But in another sense, since its inquiries ceaselessly grow in number, the circle containing them seems to become more and more vast; the more so as the mind is not content to perceive what is, but *supposes* what *could be,* so that reality thus discovered is engrossed in all kinds of possibilities. Thus the inquiring motion which envelops the object can appear, turn by turn, immense and narrow . . .[3]

I have here been referring to the increase in the range of expression as a sort of breakthrough, but the breakthrough is founded on a corresponding restriction of interest in the "actual," outside world: if the characters in James's novels are increasingly free and imaginative in their speculations ("what *could be*") about their world, so are they increasingly limited in their ability to alter the objective, physical conditions ("what is") of that world.

One might put it in simpler terms by saying that James is now cultivating a technique which, through its subjective emphases, focuses almost exclusively on the inner imaginative life of his center of consciousness. In Warner Berthoff's words, "the style turns richer and subtler, more fanciful and elaborate yet also more rankly colloquial. The conversation curls closer around its imaginative centers. The states of consciousness that were formerly attached to the outward data of realism now seem to well up directly and create their own data, their own 'worlds.' "[4]

As the "outward data of realism" become less prominent in James's fictive world, other interests and possibilities begin to be explored, and, as I tried to indicate in the analysis of the *Maisie* passage, the benefits in range and flexibility to James's prose can be enormous. Subsequent intensifications of

3. Georges Poulet, "Henry James," in *The Metamorphoses of the Circle,* tr. Carley Dawson and Elliott Coleman (Baltimore: Johns Hopkins Press, 1966), p. 317.
4. Warner Berthoff, "Henry James," in *The Ferment of Realism* (New York: The Free Press, 1965), p. 112.

image, metaphor, and emotional tone in James's fiction can be traced to the same technique. In his later work James is experimenting with and refining methods that will express adequately the kind of life—with its density and delicacy of relationships—that he values most. *Roderick Hudson, Washington Square,* and *The Portrait of a Lady* can be seen in this connection as monuments to the failure of human relationships to square with an imagined ideal. The language, gestures, and behavior of characters in those novels are crude and barbaric when contrasted with the expectations cherished by Rowland Mallet, Catherine Sloper, and Isabel Archer.

But with *The Spoils of Poynton* James begins to develop ways of actually embodying, not merely yearning for, the richer language, gestures, and behavior. Rather than emphasize the melodramatic, satirically presented deceptions (as he did in the earlier novels), he now shifts his focus to the romantic, poetically rendered illusions themselves. This is accomplished by projecting his story from the vantage point of his superior characters' imagination. Cut off from the thin and impoverished actualities and placed within the protagonists' constantly embroidering minds, the reader shares in the very process of their speculations. All the impossibly rich nuances of human relationships—relationships lifted to the complexity and the fine intelligibility of art—which are denied by real experience are consonant with the activity of the romantic imagination. The real, of course, is waiting in abeyance: James's later novels (like *The Ambassadors*) never conclude without a final reckoning. But the process of imagining—be it beautiful or fearful (as in "The Turn of the Screw")—is what engrosses our attention, and the vision thus projected, though ultimately unsupported by experience, is able to accommodate all the subtlety and interconnectedness, all the "meaning" that James vainly demanded from "clumsy Life."[5]

5. James uses this phrase in his Preface to *The Spoils of Poynton* (James, *Art of the Novel,* p. 121); I return to it later in my chapter on *The Sacred Fount.*

What Maisie Knew is James's first novel to embody these new ways of representing imagination and experience, and one important generalization should at least be mentioned now (it will be elaborated later): Maisie must imagine the real nature of the drama of the four main adults in her life because, whatever she may know, she does *not* know, could not yet know, the experience of sexual desire. She knows a good deal about it, and this of course constitutes the great charm of the novel—that delightful fusion of innocence and knowledge that characterizes the tone of Maisie's mind and is so perfectly conveyed by the tone of the narrator. Like Nanda, Strether, and Milly, she comes to know *about* everything, while remaining, as do the others, in some essential way innocent.

Several recent critics, notably Harris Wilson, Oscar Cargill, and John C. McCloskey, have rejected the more traditional reading of Maisie's innocence. In general they argue that, because she never escapes from her corrupt environment, she develops along the lines of her decadent and self-seeking parents. This interpretation is founded largely on two problematic observations: that Maisie, as the story progresses, seems indeed to know about everything and that her final offer to Sir Claude is, at best, ambiguous and, at worst, a rather tawdry attempt to replace Mrs. Beale in Sir Claude's affections (thus Mrs. Beale's shock and sense of scandal [361] at Maisie's words). I hope, in challenging the "revisionists," to indicate the very limited and special way in which Maisie "knows" what she knows, as well as to shed light on the peculiar blend of innocence and boldness in her final offer. This task is facilitated by the excellent articles that Tony Tanner, Joseph Hynes, and Edward Wasiolek have written about *What Maisie Knew*.[6]

6. Harris W. Wilson, "What *Did* Maisie Know?" *College English,* 17 (February 1956), 279–282; Oscar Cargill, *The Novels of Henry James* (New York: Macmillan, 1961), pp. 244–262; John C. McCloskey, "What Maisie Knows: A Study of Childhood and Adolescence," *American Literature,* 36 (January 1965), 485–513; Tony Tanner, *The Reign of Wonder* (New York: Cambridge University Press, 1965), pp. 278–298; Joseph

Before looking at Maisie herself, it would help to fill out the contours of her world in order to see what her achievement of an identity on its terms would entail. The following distinction between the objective world in *What Maisie Knew* and the child's way of perceiving that world—the activity of her imagination—is incomplete. We are largely shown the adult world through Maisie's eyes, and the objective world is often indistinguishable from the subjective rendering of it. This section focuses on the thing seen; later emphasis is on the process of seeing.

The first elements of the outside world that are encountered are the divorce courts: the father "bespattered from head to foot"(3); the mother even "more regarded as showing the spots"(3); the vulgarity of a public squabble. Exposure is rampant; Ida, in going out, "produced everywhere a sense of having been seen often, the sense indeed of a kind of abuse of visibility"(8), while Beale's finest attribute is "the eternal glitter of the teeth that his long mustache had been trained not to hide"(8). Physical attributes (like Ida's bosom[86]) are not all that are exposed. Miss Overmore, having deserted Ida for Beale while remaining Maisie's governess, resists vigorously any talk of a second governess: "She was in a false position and so freely and loudly called attention to it that it seemed to become almost a source of glory"(36). Nothing, it seems, is private; Mrs. Wix appears, and two pages later we read: "Every one knew the straighteners; every one knew the diadem and the button, the scallops and satin bands; every one, though Maisie had never betrayed her, knew even Clara Matilda"(25–26).

Void of privacy, the world of *Maisie* is filled with violent motion and images. At every turn Maisie is pushed, pulled, hurled between her parents like a "little feathered shuttle-cock"(14). War imagery permeates the novel. The divorce case is the "shock of battle"(3–4), she is "in the thick of the fight"(9), she has a habit "of seeing herself in discussion and finding in the fury of it—she had had a glimpse of the game of football—a sort of compensation for the doom of a peculiar passivity"(107). Violence is always breaking out before her; when she and Mrs. Beale spot her father and Mrs. Cuddon at the Exhibition, a sort of explosion occurs: "What followed was extraordinarily rapid—a minute of livelier battle than had ever yet, in so short a span at least, been waged round our heroine"(173). And when she reopens at Boulogne her dispute with Mrs. Wix, the latter "gave the jerk of a sleeper awakened or the start even of one who hears a bullet whiz at the flag of truce"(271).

These images are reinforced by the myriad abrupt and coercive gestures made toward Maisie. Smoke is blown in her face, her calves are pinched, she must sit on knees and light cigarettes, she is "pulled hither and thither and kissed"(10). Her unwilling separation from Mrs. Wix is described in the painful analogy of a tooth being extracted from a gum without the benefit of chloroform (29). The most recurrent of such oppressive gestures is the embrace. Ostensibly a promise of security and affection, in *Maisie* (as in *The Portrait of a Lady, The Bostonians,* and *The Golden Bowl*) it more often implies smothering appropriation.

The adult social world of *What Maisie Knew* and the other late novels is flooded with gestures of affection, but the feeling behind the gesture is often impossible to discern or rely upon. As Maisie learns at Kensington Gardens, the embrace can have unexpected consequences:

. . . her mother opened a pair of arms of extraordinary elegance, and then she felt the loosening of his [Sir Claude's] grasp. "My own child," Ida murmured in a voice—a voice of sudden confused tenderness—that it seemed to her she heard for the first time.

She wavered but an instant, thrilled with the first direct appeal, as distinguished from the mere maternal pull, she had ever had from lips that . . . had always been sharp. The next moment she was on her mother's breast, where, amid a wilderness of trinkets, she felt as if she had suddenly been thrust, with a smash of glass, into a jeweler's shop-front, but only to be as suddenly ejected with a push and the brisk injunction: "Now go to the Captain!"[145].

Moved by the promise of real affection, Maisie entrusts herself to Ida's embrace, but the maternal bosom is gaudy and dehumanized, "a wilderness of trinkets." Moreover, between her and the implied affection there is, as it were, an unseen plate of glass, the barrier of discrepancy between the gesture and the sought-for private reality it promises; into this glass Maisie crashes, discovering that she is still estranged from genuine intimacy.

Her estrangement is on two other occasions rendered by the same image of the pane of glass,[7] and, as in the earlier figure of the passive spectator at the furious football game, Maisie is constantly on the verge of, and yet isolated from, the intimacies and passions of the adult world. This kind of exclusion, this sense of being always at a remove from one's experience not only permeates *The Sacred Fount* and "In the Cage," but it is analogous to the fate of the Jamesian novelist, who is also separated from the intimacies and passions he must view from a distance, observing and mentally delineating from the cage of the imagination the experience he does not otherwise share.

The embrace, at all events, is not to be trusted, which introduces another major characteristic of Maisie's world: its decep-

7. Cf. the following: "[her] sharpened sense of spectatorship . . . gave her often an odd air of being present at her history in as separate a manner as if she could only get at experience by flattening her nose against a pane of glass"(107). "She was to feel henceforth as if she were flattening her nose upon the hard window pane of the sweet-shop of knowledge"(137).

tive artifice. The artifice is an effect of appearances not indicating, for her, any reliable reality. The mad antics that Maisie observes strike her as a game, "a collection of images and echoes to which meanings were attachable—images and echoes kept for her in the childish dusk . . . like games she wasn't yet big enough to play"(12). This motif is furthered by the "ever so many games in boxes"(71) that Sir Claude gives Maisie and Mrs. Wix, games "to while away the evening hour," the instructions to which the two females never succeed in deciphering.

Experience, for Maisie, becomes just such an indecipherable game; everyone's maneuvers are inscrutable counters. Miss Overmore sees Mrs. Wix's visit as "a game like another," her visit being "clearly the first move in it"(52). Beale informs Maisie that she's "a jolly good pretext . . . for their [Sir Claude and Mrs. Beale's] game"(189); Sir Claude frets over Ida's apparent kindness to Mrs. Wix, wondering "what Ida is *really* up to, what game she was playing . . ."(245). And Mrs. Wix triumphantly pronounces on Mrs. Beale's Boulogne strategy: "Oh she's cruelly clever! It's not a moral sense . . . It's a game!"(297). Perhaps the best gloss for the meaning of this recurrent motif appears during the remarkable scene in Kensington Gardens, when Maisie, believing that the Captain really does love Ida, discovers that, by comparison, Sir Claude does not: "Mrs. Wix's original account of Sir Claude's affection seemed as empty now as the chorus in a children's game"(152).

The violent machinations of the adult world, pointing to no recognizable reality of feelings, seem mysterious, self-interested designs in which others are to be exploited as fully as possible. As Mrs. Beale says humorously of Sir Claude: "I'll pick him to the bone!"(126). Although the Captain's display of feeling for Ida, while partly comic, pierces Maisie with its clarity, she is more often confused: "Everything had something behind it: life was like a long, long corridor with rows of closed doors. She had learned that at these doors it was wise not to knock—this seemed to produce from within such sounds of derision"(33–34). The passage is salient, both lightly echoing a passage in *The Portrait of a Lady* and anticipating the very structure of *The Sacred Fount,* as well as foreshadowing the exotic image of the closed pagoda in *The Golden Bowl.*[8] The doors at which Maisie has learned not to knock are, of course, those to which I have repeatedly referred, the barriers to intimacy and passion, and the passage points to the role of imagination in Maisie's life, the unique way in which she manages to read and misread her world.

The particular innocence of Maisie that I would insist upon derives simply from the fact that she has no personal experience of certain human passions, and that "she was taken into the confidence of passions on which she fixed just the stare she might have had for images bounding across the wall in the slide of a magic lantern. Her little world was phantasmagoric—strange shadows dancing on a sheet"(9). This sense of phantasmagoria is rendered, for the reader, largely by the abrupt, violent images and gestures in Maisie's world, by her passive immersion in something like a football game. She does not learn to play, but by dint of intense concentration she begins to understand how others play and the "value" of their moves. She never swerves, however, from her "belief that the

8. "With all her love of knowledge she had a natural shrinking from curtains and looking into unlighted corners. The love of knowledge coexisted in her mind with the finest capacity for ignorance." (James, *Portrait of a Lady,* I,284.) I quote only the end of the pagoda passage; after Maggie has noted its exotic, inscrutable presence, squarely within "the garden of her life," she approaches. "She had knocked, in short—though she could scarce have said whether for admission or for what; she had applied her hand to a cool, smooth spot, and had waited to see what would happen. Something *had* happened; it was as if a sound, at her touch, after a little, had come back to her from within; a sound sufficiently suggesting that her approach had been noted." (James, *The Golden Bowl* [New York: Scribner's, 1909], II,4.)

grown-up time was the time of real amusement and above all of real intimacy"(55–56). Real intimacy and the certitude of experiential knowledge are denied her, but, in their absence, she manages to acquire an expert familiarity with surface motions and imaginatively to intuit the meanings beneath them.

In this restricted sense Maisie learns to live in her world. After blurting out to mamma "that you're a nasty horrid pig!"(13), she realizes, through mamma's presumable reaction, that such messages are better concealed than delivered. Hereafter she stores within herself these bits of surface knowledge: keeping mamma's and papa's insults from each other, Mrs. Beale's fondness for Sir Claude and his for her from Ida, Sir Claude's visits to Mrs. Beale from Mrs. Wix, Clara Matilda from everyone, and—even—the Captain's feeling for Ida from Sir Claude.

She learns that the adults about her constantly seek to square one another and that this is done "by letting him do what he wants on condition that he lets you also do it"(128). At the brown lady's apartment, her developed powers of imaginative observation are fully displayed. Through Beale's nervous fidgeting and pats on the back, she is able to penetrate beyond his words and discern that he not only intends to bolt without her but that "what he wanted, hang it, was that she should let him off with all the honours—with all the appearance of virtue and sacrifice on his side"(187). Finally, at Boulogne, her sophisticated precociousness leads her to admonish Mrs. Wix: "Yes, I see what you mean. But at that time they weren't free . . . I don't think you know how free they've become"(273).

Such a remark, with its unintentional play on "free," conveys the peculiar confines of Maisie's knowledge. Freedom, her limited experience and extensive perceptions tell her, refers only to their newfound opportunity to take care of her, as they are now free of their former burden. But Maisie is ignorant (innocent) of the sexual connotation of the word and, thereby, of the entire moral issue Mrs. Wix tries so strenuously to raise. Maisie can judge but by surfaces and her meager empirical knowledge; once Sir Claude's and Mrs. Beale's relations are abstracted or considered in the light of moral systems, they have no meaning for her. She is aware only of the concrete way their "freedom" affects her, and at this point it seems something to be welcomed. Consequently, when Mrs. Wix attempts to crush Maisie's argument by "explaining," with "a sidelong squint," the connection between Mrs. Cuddon and Beale: "She pays him!" Maisie responds, "Oh *does* she? . . . I don't say she's not generous"(273–274).

Her inability to judge morally squalid events within a received moral framework is what constitutes Maisie's unflagging "freshness" and what gives to all her "knowledge" the charm and wonder (which James later admired in his Preface) of her innocent imagination. In the largest sense the novel is a study of subjective, imaginative perception insofar as that marvelous tone of uncomprehending innocence pronounces on matters to us most squalid. The more she "knows," the more we see how little, in *our* sense, she knows, which is to say, the more complete is the distinction between her "naïve" knowledge born of observation and vicarious imagination, and our adulterated knowledge born of personal, shared experience or received social norms. It is now necessary to examine her development into maturity, those formative movements of contact between her subjective vision and needs, on the one hand, and the objective facts of her world, on the other.[9] These moments, as with Isabel, constitute the core of her personal experience and are crucial to our understanding of her final decision.

9. One of the big differences, pointed out by Marius Bewley in *The Complex Fate* (London: Chatto and Windus, 1952), between *What Maisie Knew* and *The Sacred Fount* is that in the former one can still distinguish between subjective and objective worlds, while in the latter one cannot.

The first serious development within Maisie, the first major assessment of her world, comes when she discovers that she has been used by each parent as a vessel to carry insults to the other. This occasions "the comple vision, private but final, of the strange office she filled. It was literally a moral revolution and accomplished in the depths of her nature"(15). Hereafter she feigns stupidity, and though her awareness of her environment is constantly increasing and altering her views, her mind seems made up about her parents. She calmly tells Sir Claude: "Mamma doesn't care for me . . . Not really"(83).

One must interpret Maisie's drama against this background of disintegrating familial confidence and security. Deprived of certitude in her most basic relationships, Maisie is shuttled from person to person and from event to event, patiently attempting to get her bearings straight. The instability of what one would assume to be the most intransigent reality—one's own parentage—is conveyed by Mrs. Beale's verbal gymnastics, as she blithely announces her new marriage to the astonished Maisie and Mrs. Wix: "He's my husband, if you please, and I'm his little wife. So *now* we'll see who's your little mother!"(51). The singsong rhythm of Mrs. Beale's words, as she casually juggles with equations conventionally the least manipulable, has a dizzying effect, and it is echoed by the unsteady merry-go-round image of the prancing horse in the following passage: "Their companion [Maisie] gazed from one of them to the other, thinking that though she had been happy indeed between Sir Claude and Mrs. Wix she should evidently be happier still between Sir Claude and Mrs. Beale. But it was like being perched on a prancing horse, and she made a movement to hold on to something. 'Then, you know, shan't I bid good-bye to Mrs. Wix?' "(132).

The first substitute for her parents is Miss Overmore, and, in response to the latter's apparent affection, Maisie "conceived her first passion, and the object of it was her governess"(22). But the relationship proves unreliable; she is inexplicably separated from Miss Overmore and shoved into Mrs. Wix's embrace. Parting from Mrs. Wix proves to have all the pain of the dental analogy mentioned earlier, and insofar as Maisie remains baffled before the mysterious laws of her parents' world, she will remain emotionally uprooted.

When Sir Claude appears, she makes him the center of her life, its primary source of stability. He stands solid in her world of phantasmagoric images and becomes the recipient of those feelings her parents have failed to nurture and reciprocate. This frustrated emotion, usually concealed, emerges unexpectedly on several occasions, and it erupts most poignantly not with Sir Claude but in the scene with the Captain in Kensington Gardens:

She was fairly hushed with the sense that he spoke of her mother as she had never heard anyone speak. It came over her as she sat silent that, after all, this admiration and this respect were quite new words . . . What it appeared to her to come to was that on the subject of her ladyship it was the first real kindness she had heard, so that at the touch of it something strange and deep and pitying surged up within her—a revelation that, practically and so far as she knew, her mother, apart from this, had only been disliked . . . The tears filled her eyes and rolled down her cheeks . . . She became on the spot indifferent to her usual fear of showing what in children was notoriously most offensive—presented to her companion, soundlessly but hideously, her wet distorted face. She cried, with a pang, straight *at* him, cried as she had never cried at anyone in all her life. "Oh do you love her?" she brought out with a gulp which was the effect of her trying not to make a noise[151–152].

The Captain is only a minor character, but this is, for me, the most powerful scene in the novel. For a moment the reader is plunged without warning into the depths of Maisie's emotional turmoil. The pathos of her response to these first warm words about her mother is increased by the tacit parallel to her own case, and her pity begins to be flooded with self-pity as she cries "Oh do you love her?" For a moment the game is transcended, and Maisie responds to the genuine feeling in the Captain. She is open with him as with no others; comically and movingly she implores him to be faithful:

"You *do* love her?"
"My dear child—!" The Captain wanted words.
"Then don't do it only for just a little."
"A little?"
"Like all the others."
"All the others?"—he stood staring.
She pulled away her hand. "Do it always!"[155].

The parallel with her own case is explicit now, as the desire for love and security for her mother merges with her own yearnings. The scene gives a measure of Maisie's emotional needs—things barely mentioned in the book but implicit throughout—and explains why Maisie is later able to see her parents as still potentially affectionate, though her mind, more detached, perceptive, and educated than her frustrated emotions, can judge them with greater accuracy. Furthermore, it gives a measure of the intensity of Maisie's dream of living with Sir Claude, the one on whom, finally, she has staked the most of herself.

As she grows up, however, and learns in her deprived state to infer the pattern from the piece, her expert familiarity with surfaces finds increasing qualifications in the security and love Sir Claude offers. Quite early she discovers that he lies to her, and, as she becomes more discerning, she can interpret his fidgeting and hesitations: "there was something that touched her in the embarrassed, almost humiliated way their companion's [Mrs. Wix's] challenge made him turn it round and round. She had seen people do that who, she was sure, did nothing else that Sir Claude did" (249).

Another deterrent to Maisie's dream of self-fulfillment is her awareness of the risk of Ida's and Beale's unrestricted egotism—the risk of being a "low sneak." This phrase continues to glow in her mind, and it gives her pause when she first considers dropping Mrs. Wix for a life of proposed beatitude with her stepparents: "She wondered if she herself shouldn't be a low sneak in learning to be so happy without Mrs. Wix"(134). Likewise, when she reflects on Mrs. Wix's plan of excluding Mrs. Beale, the phrase stubbornly returns to mind: "She enjoyed in a word an ineffaceable view of the fact that there were things papa called mamma and mamma called papa a low sneak for doing or for not doing. Now this rich memory gave her a name that she dreaded to invite to the lips of Mrs. Beale"(270). Either action seems petty, self-interested, and cruel to the one excluded. Listening to the civil "Adieu, mesdames!" of an old French woman, and glimpsing for a moment the finer French manner in which courtesy might be part of morality, Maisie speaks against the rudeness of Mrs. Wix's proposed exclusion: "Why after all should we have to choose between you? Why shouldn't we be four?"(271). Her sense of morality, at this point, is based entirely on her surface view of the concrete cases before her, not on a priori conceptual codes. Without having to be a low sneak, she wonders naïvely, why shouldn't they all four be able to live more pleasurably together than apart?

Only in the last chapter do these motifs culminate, and Maisie's need for security runs headlong into her dispassionate, now quite perceptive, view of the world about her, thus precipitating her single climactic decision. Nervous and embarrassed, Sir Claude issues his proposal: to drop Mrs. Wix and live, the three of them, together. Like Goodwood in *The Portrait*, but with less conviction, Sir Claude argues that the world is large and they can begin again. Maisie understands clearly that, for him, "if Mrs. Wix clung it was all the more reason for shaking Mrs. Wix off"(337). Faced with this appeal, Maisie feels terror, "and it seemed to her that suddenly she knew, as she knew it about Sir Claude, what she was afraid of. She was afraid of herself"(338).

Maisie's motives, in this scene and in what follows, are admittedly difficult to assess. Although her temptation is ostensibly to flee with Sir Claude and later join Mrs. Beale, thereby betraying Mrs. Wix, the scene is strangely intense and ambiguous. For what is oppressively latent though never mentioned between them is their mutual desire to escape to the South, leaving the governess and the stepmother stranded together in the North. Thus, though they discuss whether Maisie can bear to sacrifice Mrs. Wix, they are actually exploring—through fearful, penetrating glances at each other and obsessive meanderings toward the railroad station and the docks—the possibility of embarking on a life together. But as the train for Paris and the great world finally leaves the Boulogne station, something crucial happens: "She had had a real fright but had fallen back to earth. The odd thing was that in her fall her fear too had been dashed down and broken. It was gone. She looked round at last . . . at Sir Claude's, and then saw that his wasn't"(345).

Two options, then—one explicit and one implicit—have been before her during this scene, but in the passage just quoted, the fall "back to earth" effectively indicates her awareness that they are both dead options: the train is gone. At this moment, disregarding altogether Sir Claude's proposal, she rises to her situation and articulates her desire. The first option—three of them together and one "dropped"—has been bandied about by the novel ever since the principal conflicts emerged, and Maisie now discards it permanently. In expressing her desire she realizes immediately, perhaps even before she speaks, that Sir Claude will be unequal to it: " 'Oh!' he exclaimed, on which she saw how much, how hopelessly he was afraid . . . Mrs. Wix was right. He was afraid of his weakness—of his weakness"(346).

She makes the proposal, knowing, I believe, that, though the chance of acceptance is unlikely, she still must make it. It is the right offer because, unlike the earlier option, it resolves two concerns that the novel has persistently presented as mutually incompatible: parental and sexual interests.

Maisie resolves these two in her proposal not because she seeks to be his lover, but because she finally senses the configuration of her own experience. She senses what has always been the case but what her feeling for Sir Claude has hitherto prevented her from recognizing: that, insofar as he is Mrs. Beale's lover, he cannot give her the relationship she needs—not for abstract reasons but because his dependence on Mrs. Beale makes him unreliable and devious with Maisie. It comes down to a special quality of caring for someone, a quality so intense that it cannot be divided into sexual and affectionate components—the kind of caring Maisie seemed to descry in the Captain. This quality of feeling, with the love and security it promises, Maisie now knows she cannot win from Sir Claude. His sexual attachment, though he feels less fondly about it, runs more deeply; it is incompatible both with Maisie's desire and with what he would wish to offer her (thus his embarrassment over his proposal and his pride in her refusal). If she cannot go with him and Mrs. Beale, it is because she realizes that any relationship among the three of them will be—and, by implication, has always been—ambiguous and deficient. As Joseph Hynes remarks in his excellent analysis of the novel, "she arrives at a knowledge of certain human combinations that are simply unworkable, though she remains innocent of certain specific reasons for the unworkability."[10] This is, moreover, exactly what the novel has been patiently showing us, with our greater awareness, to be the facts of Maisie's situation, though until now she herself has not seen her case in the same light or with the same clarity.

In other words, her proposal is an implicit judgment and rejection of the muddled parental-sexual relations that have heretofore made up her world. She wants something simpler

10. Hynes, "Middle Way of Miss Farange," p. 545. This is perhaps the most thorough study yet made of the novel. Although I believe Hynes slights the sexual theme and somewhat overestimates Sir Claude, he is still immensely persuasive in his nuanced reading of Maisie's innocence.

and more inclusive, and, though James has no words to describe the relationship she seeks, he does tell us that Sir Claude's look at Maisie "simply meant that he knew all she herself meant"(347). Sir Claude knows, and knows himself to be unequal to such a need; that is, he is "afraid of his weakness." This could mean either that he fears his sexual dependence on Mrs. Beale or his sexual dependence on women in general (we have seen his promiscuous glances throughout the novel), or even that he fears his relationship with the adolescent Maisie might degenerate to a sordid, sexual basis. What is common to all these fears, it seems to me, is his awareness of his own sexuality which, as it were, disqualifies him from accepting Maisie's innocent offer. It disqualifies him because, as in so much of James's fiction, moral irresponsibility and sexual activity are obscurely linked.

If Sir Claude had accepted the offer, then Maisie could have been accused of being a low sneak to both Mrs. Beale and Mrs. Wix, perhaps a less nasty charge than being a low sneak to only one of them. However, her relationship with Sir Claude alone, by eliminating the sexual-parental confusion caused by Mrs. Beale's presence, would have obviated much of Mrs. Wix's reproach. His acceptance would, moreover, have indicated his caring most for her in the same way she cares most for him; there would at least have been that relational clarity and wholeness within a novel of unusual emotional disorientation. For Maisie is now expressing actively and unambiguously her deepest feelings. Love and security are what, all her life, she has been unsuccessful in attaining, and she now sees that there is only one way to have them. Sir Claude's design, as she comes to realize through her increasing perception of the deviousness of his past relationship with her and Mrs. Beale, cannot work; he hardly believes in it himself. Hence, she rises to her awareness and articulates her need, not competing with her stepmother on a sexual plane but making it clear that the kind of love she desires and wishes to

94

offer is incompatible with the sexual love Sir Claude feels for Mrs. Beale. He must choose.

But Maisie has not waited this long, has not assessed Sir Claude so closely, has not watched the train leave for Paris and fallen back to earth herself, only to make an offer which, if believed in entirely, demonstrably "overrates" Sir Claude and resurrects the hope for escape she has just dashed. The offer is a clarification, not a new development, of her situation; it is made with utter seriousness but with little hope of acceptance. It puts things in their real perspective: if she can't have love from him as intense and unfragmented as the Captain's for Ida, then she won't have him at all.

She now knows what she wants, and she sees how little any arrangement but her own can meet her desire. Her certitude comes, finally, from her first real knowledge: from expecting nothing and from realizing that his world—the social sexual world—has never given her what she needs, and that she cannot have him without accepting his world: " 'Will *you* come? Won't you?' she enquired as if she had not already seen that she should have to give him up. It was the last flare of her dream. By this time she was afraid of nothing"(352).

There is something courageous, as well as self-interested, in Maisie's finally expressing herself: she selfishly deserts Mrs. Wix and Mrs. Beale to have Sir Claude for herself, but she bravely seeks, under considerable pressure, the kind of love her entire experience has hitherto denied her. Even more courageous is her willingness to run such a risk to have him the right way or not at all. Mrs. Wix, for all her dubious characteristics both moral and emotional—and I agree with those critics like Marius Bewley and Tony Tanner who stress them—will provide Maisie with more security and stability than the two charming lovers.

With this decision the motifs of oppressive embraces and war imagery reach their crescendo and subside. Mrs. Wix and Mrs. Beale furiously try to pull her into their camp, but the salient image is that of Sir Claude "resting his hands very lightly on her shoulders and facing the loud adversaries"(358), claiming softly that "she's free—she's free"(359). And she does choose her destiny; that James knew how to distinguish a free choice from a forced one is clear once one contrasts Maisie's departure with that of the smothered, tearful, confused Verena Tarrant in *The Bostonians*. It is Maisie, not Mrs. Wix, who says, "Shan't we lose the boat?"(362). After they catch the steamer, their fears and emotions gradually subside, and the last view of them, "in mid-channel, surrounded by the quiet sea"(363), suggests a serenity long sought and finally attained.

But if the peace thus attained represents an achieved victory, a poised acceptance, this victory and acceptance also imply a considerable exclusion. Maisie ultimately perceives the adult world of sexual passion and intimacy, of self-interest and exploitation of others, as being uninhabitable. Her most basic needs go unanswered in the great world, and she calmly chooses, instead, another outsider equally isolated, Mrs. Wix. Symbolically, one cannot help noting, here as in *The Awkward Age,* the socially and sexually attractive male—the one who promises the richer experience of intimacy and love—proves defective. The heroine who is just entering sexual maturity is left only with an elderly friend who is beyond it; clearsighted, deprived, and uprooted, Maisie is left with little more than the dubious Mrs. Wix and her own imaginative capacities. Meager as they are, however, even these comforts are unavailable to the next Jamesian hero we examine: the unidentified and exasperating narrator of *The Sacred Fount*.

IV The Exploitative and Protective Imagination: Aspects of the Artist in *The Sacred Fount*

What I wanted, in my presumption, was that the object, the place, the person, the unreduced impression . . . should give out to me something of a situation.

　　　　　　　　　　　　　　Henry James, Autobiography

This necessity I was under that everything should be interesting . . .

　　　　　　　　　　　　　　Henry James, Autobiography

IT IS BEST TO CONCEDE at the outset that there are compelling reasons for not discussing *The Sacred Fount*. Like "The Turn of the Screw" (and, indeed, like *The Mystery of Edwin Drood*), *The Sacred Fount* has received critical attention beyond the intrinsic merits of the book, attention mainly attracted by the novel's undeniable mystery and its haunting biographical relevance. Although much of this criticism suffers from aimlessness or overingenuity, there remains a body of penetrating interpretations sufficient to discourage yet another "explanation" of what *The Sacred Fount* is really about. It seems safe to say both that the novel is founded on enough ambiguities to prevent any interpretation from being authoritative and that the disagreements are fundamental enough to suggest that, beyond the possible motes in the eyes of the critics, there is something unsound, in conception or realization, about the *Fount* itself.

Nevertheless, any study centering on the meanings of imagination and experience in James's fiction must acknowledge *The Sacred Fount* as an indispensable text. Analogies suggested earlier between Rowland Mallet and the novelist, between Gilbert Osmond and Ralph Touchett and the novelist, pale before the gigantic, the really unavoidable analogy between the narrator of the *Fount* and the novelist (thus justifying the suspicion of a "haunting biographical relevance"). Whatever else the novel may be about, it depicts the frustrated attempt of the observer-artist-narrator to maintain his "exquisite" theory of relationships among the recalcitrant elements of Newmarch society who make up those relationships. Or, to put it in the terms of my argument, the novel depicts James's most sustained exploration of the relation between a character's imagination and his experience.

Approaches to the *Fount,* however, are beset with dangers, the most prominent of which is the attempt to define exactly "what happens" in the book in order to solve its mystery. This is tantamount to seeking (fruitlessly) to identify the "unnamed article" manufactured by the Newsomes in *The Ambassadors;* James took pains to make the article unidentifiable, and he took even greater pains to make the *Fount* ambiguous. Any interpretation that dispels the ambiguity, therefore, is doomed to superficiality, and I am interested here in explaining the confusion rather than explaining it away.

There are several specific reasons why a definitive interpretation is impossible. As Jean F. Blackall points out in her book on the *Fount,* two incompletely united subjects, with their respective conflicting tones, exist side by side: "The original subject—the 'vampire' *donnée*—gradually became for James subsidiary to the mind of the character who conceives it."[1] The somber, portentous passages in the novel convey the weighty "original subject," while the passages of high comedy are appropriate to the social adventure of the bumbling narrator.

1. Jean Frantz Blackall, *Jamesian Ambiguity and* The Sacred Fount (Ithaca, N.Y.: Cornell University Press, 1965), p. 15.

The consequent difficulty for the reader is to make sense of a narrative voice whose tone can fluctuate between poetic meditation and unintentional self-mockery.

Consider, for example, the solemn intensity of the narrator's reflection, as he is walking along the grounds and thinking about the doomed May Server: "The last calls of birds sounded extraordinarily loud; they were like the timed, serious splashes, in wide, still water, of divers not expecting to rise again."[2] The same narrator, however, is capable of a distinctively different, comic tone, as heard in the following hubristic reflection after Lady John's attack: "*I* alone was magnificently and absurdly aware—everyone else was benightedly out of it"(139). Mrs. Blackall notices the confusion caused by these two tones, but she resolves the problem rather too easily, I think, by emphasizing the comedy and labeling the narrator's sacred fount theory merely pathological. Although I argue later the error of this approach, her book remains a perceptive and detailed study of the novel, a mine of information about the problems it presents.

A second source of ambiguity is that all of the *Fount* is told in the first person by an unidentified narrator who displays some very suspicious traits. The novel's opening sentence shows him on the lookout for "possible friends and even possible enemies"; he hopes there may be "happy ambiguities." Moreover, his original low estimation of Long—a kernel of his subsequent theory—is subjectively based on questionable evidence: "he [Long] had always, in the interval, so failed to know me that I could only hold him as stupid unless I held him as impertinent"(3). Long "recognizes" the narrator on the train to Newmarch, and the elaborate theoretical edifice that fol-

2. Henry James, *The Sacred Fount* (London: Macmillan, 1923), p. 101. Subsequent quotations from *The Sacred Fount* refer to this edition (Volume XXIX of *The Novels and Stories of Henry James: New and Complete Edition*); hereafter, all page references will be included within the text, parenthetically, after the quotation. In slightly different form, this chapter has appeared in *Harvard English Studies* 1, ed. Morton W. Bloomfield (Cambridge, Mass: Harvard University Press, 1970), pp. 189–209.

lows—the "explanation" of Long's newly acquired intelligence—can arguably be attributed to this boost to the narrator's ego.

Even more suspicious are some aspects of his technique: he tends to finish others' sentences for them and to interpret their questions in the light of his own cogitations. When Mrs. Briss asks him if he "then regarded Gilbert Long as now exalted to the position of the most brilliant of our companions"(31), he takes it as a personal challenge and responds, "Hardly that, perhaps—for don't you see the proofs I'm myself giving you?" He then qualifies the estimate of Long as "the cleverest but one." But the egotistic, theory-obsessed narrator may have entirely missed the drift of Mrs. Briss's question; as Mrs. Blackall notes, ". . . a much more obvious meaning for her question would be, do you really think Gilbert Long is as brilliant as all that?"[3]

The most equivocal of the techniques at the service of his theory is his way of handling apparently discrepant observations. When May Server seems innocently surprised by his "knowing" disclosure of "poor Briss's" interest in her, the narrator at first acknowledges this as a threat to "the whole airy structure," but then rapidly converts the menace into support: "I quickly saw in it, from the moment I had got my point of view, more fine things than ever. I saw for instance that, magnificently, she wished not to incriminate him"(113). This conversion technique infuriates many critics, and Maxwell Geismar accordingly fulminates: "He becomes the perfect proto-Freudian analyst, as it were, who is always right, who always understands the peculiar behavior of the 'patients' who may oppose or flatly deny his speculations; the analyst who can rationalize away any action which contradicts his own 'conclusions.' "[4]

3. Blackall, *Jamesian Ambiguity,* p. 47.
4. Maxwell Geismar, *Henry James and the Jacobites* (Boston: Houghton Mifflin, 1963), p. 208.

With these hazards to interpretation in mind, one may question the wisdom of seriously examining the narrator at all. The reason for doing so, I believe, is that in his ambiguous and suspect nature he embodies a profound, if skeptical, version of the artist himself at work, and his theory—as unreliable as it may be—entails a process of verification and posits a view of experience that are essential elements in James's fictive world.

Before exploring this theory and developing more fully the analogy between the narrator and the novelist, I should say that the analogy was first proposed by Wilson Follett, has been more or less accepted by Edmund Wilson, R. P. Blackmur, and Laurence Holland, but has been questioned or rejected by critics as knowledgeable as Leon Edel, Oscar Cargill, and Jean F. Blackall. These last three, if they can be united, are acutely aware of the comic and satiric elements in the *Fount;* they conclude that James never subjected himself or his art to such a critical and mocking "searchlight of irony" (Follett's phrase). I hope in the following pages to justify my contention that he did.[5]

The source of the analogy between the narrator and the novelist is that both seek to comprehend—indeed to shape—in terms of intelligible form, the experience around them:

I was just conscious, vaguely, of being on the track of a law, a law that would fit, that would strike me as governing the delicate phenomena—delicate though so marked—that my imagination found itself playing with. A part of the amusement they

5. Wilson Follett, "The Simplicity of Henry James," *American Review,* 1 (May-June 1923), 315–325; Edmund Wilson, "The Ambiguity of Henry James," in *The Triple Thinkers,* rev. ed. (New York: Oxford University Press, 1963), pp. 88–132; R. P. Blackmur, *"The Sacred Fount,"* *Kenyon Review,* 4 (Autumn 1942), 328–352; Laurence B. Holland, *The Expense of Vision: Essays on the Craft of Henry James* (Princeton, N.J.: Princeton University Press, 1964), pp. 183–226; Leon Edel, "An Introductory Essay," in *The Sacred Fount* (New York: Grove Press, 1953), pp. v–xxxii; Oscar Cargill, *The Novels of Henry James* (New York: Macmillan, 1961), pp. 280–299.

yielded came, I daresay, from my exaggerating them—grouping them into a larger mystery (and thereby a larger "law") than the facts, as observed, yet warranted; but that is the common fault of minds for which the vision of life is an obsession. The obsession pays, if one will; but to pay it has to borrow[19–20].

The passage bristles with implications; through its various vocabularies of hunting, amusement, obsession, and finance, it suggests something of the complexity of the narrator's behavior. Rather than lazily accepting his experience in conventional, "ready-made" patterns, the narrator sees the phenomena about him as essentially mysterious, and his imagination seeks tirelessly—one might even say ferociously—to interpret that experience (those phenomena) within comprehensive, all-explaining laws. If this is amusement, it is also obsession. Furthermore, in the very act of ordering his experience into a pattern, the narrator is aware that he exaggerates, aggrandizes the phenomena he is to explain. He makes more of their wonder than "the facts, as observed," warrant: he transforms what may really only be discrepant observations into the more interesting seams of a patterned story. And this is the distortion typical "of minds for which the vision of life is an obsession."

Like the artist, he is obsessed with the way things compose, with the figure in the carpet, with the latent story buried in phenomena that, to the untrained eye or passive imagination, seem blankly innocent. He exaggerates in the interest of form; his deepest allegiance is to "story," an imputed pattern of human relationships, richer, more throbbing and intense than appearance may actually justify. To use the phrase from the famous letter to Wells, the narrator's behavior enacts James's assertion that it is "art that *makes* life."[6] In Dorothea Krook's acceptable gloss, this means "that the artist at once creates the conditions in which life can be 'ideally' exhibited and exhibits it thus ideally by exploring and articulating the fullest

6. *The Letters of Henry James,* ed. Percy Lubbock (New York: Scribner's, 1920), II, 490.

implications of the given case. Life is made to yield its fullest, richest meanings when subjected to the artistic process."[7]

What we see in *The Sacred Fount,* however, is that the process can be an obsession and that it exacts a cost. "To pay it has to borrow," and one may hazard that it is from himself—the inmost sources of his own vitality—that the narrator's obsession borrows the energy necessary to "complete," creatively and appreciatively, the otherwise disparate phenomena of life. Thus enervated by his artistic obsession with "the vision of life," the narrator, like the novelist, cannot immerse himself in the experience of life, and this may account for his characteristic solitude and deprivation. Even if the reader grants such conjectures, however, he is likely to regret that this particular "story," this "vision of life" is actually so limited in the possibilities it invokes. The question of the appropriateness and adequacy of the sacred fount theory as a possible form for experience must be reserved until later, when I examine the theory itself more closely.

However obsessed, the narrator of *The Sacred Fount* remains aware of the possible discrepancy between any form and the experience it seeks—through shaping—to define. Descrying Mrs. Briss and Long "intensely" together ("For that was it—they *were* as one; as one, at all events, for *my* large reading") shortly after he has put Briss and May Server together, the narrator goes on to warn himself "that I mustn't take them [the two sets of couples] equally for granted merely *because* they balanced. Things in the real had a way of not balancing; it was all an affair, this fine symmetry, of artificial proportion"(143)'. And as he reflects upon the implications of seeing Mrs. Briss and Long together, he uses a significant literary metaphor:

My large reading had meanwhile, for the convenience of the rest of my little talk with Lady John, to make itself as small

7. Dorothea Krook, *The Ordeal of Consciousness in Henry James* (New York: Cambridge University Press, 1962), p. 410.

as possible. I had an odd sense, till we fell apart again, as of keeping my finger rather stiffly fixed on a passage in a favourite author on which I had not previously lighted. I held the book out of sight and behind me; I spoke of things that were not at all in it—or not at all on that particular page; but my volume, none the less, was only waiting. What might be written there hummed already in my ears as a result of my mere glimpse. Had *they* also wonderfully begun to know? Had *she*, most wonderfully, and had they, in that case, prodigiously come together on it? This was a possibility into which my imagination could dip even deeper . . . [143].

Several of the reader's impressions fall into place through the use of the book metaphor. The narrator's speculations are likened to the responses one makes to a work of fiction; correspondingly the characters he ponders over are, by analogy, at a further remove from life than he is. If the narrator is fictional, then they are the fictions of a fiction, thus comparable to literary creations of his, a possibility that several other passages in the novel seem to suggest:

I found, on my side, a rare intellectual joy, the oddest secret exultation, in feeling her [Lady John] begin instantly to play the part I had attributed to her in the irreducible drama[81].

To see all this was at the time, I remember, to be as inhumanly amused as if one had found one could create something. I had created nothing but a clue or two to the larger comprehension I still needed, yet I positively found myself overtaken by a mild artistic glow[83].

I was positively . . . proud of my work. I had thought it all out, and to have thought it was, wonderfully, to have brought it[101].

Furthermore, the "text" he is studying, like *The Sacred Fount* itself, is endlessly suggestive; the more he plumbs it, the further his imagination is stimulated and the more intricate his theory can become. Indeed, upon second and third readings the *Fount* does become a more and more complicated maze; for each cryptic appearance or remark there are several possible meanings, none ever excluded. Finally, the remove from real-ity—the distinction between literature and life—implied by the book metaphor gives point to the narrator's concern that his "fine symmetry" may be merely "artificial proportion."

Although the narrator's mind is furiously active, his actual knowledge, it becomes clear, remains meager. James renders this privation by having the narrator again and again chance upon a man and a woman together, one face forward and the other turned around. The lack of identification summons forth the tireless imagination, and at one point (65–67) the narrator and Mrs. Briss heatedly dispute for two pages the identity of such a hidden figure, arguing him to be, according to their different theories, either M. de Dreuil or Gilbert Long, until he turns around and is seen to be Briss.

The narrator then knowingly exclaims that " 'it wasn't, at all events, Gilbert Long behind the tree!' My triumph, how-ever, beneath the sponge she was prepared to pass again over much of our experience, was short-lived. 'Of course it wasn't. What could she possibly have put poor Briss there for but just to show it wasn't?' " (70). The reshaping sponge suggests the liberties taken with appearances in this novel. Both the narrator and Mrs. Briss feel free to mold experience—otherwise unintelligible and unformed—so as to fit the form of their theories. In such a scene James makes manifest what is implicit throughout the book: in the absence of information the fecund imagination constantly creates its own "facts."

Moreover, the absence of information is the chosen condition of the narrator. Throughout his Prefaces James reiterates how, once he has come upon the "germ" for a story, he must avoid hearing any more so that the imagination can play freely with its materials:

There had been but ten words, yet I had recognized in them, as in a flash, all the possibilities of the little drama of my "Spoils," which glimmered then and there into life; so that when in the next breath I began to hear of action taken, on the beautiful ground, by our engaged adversaries . . . I saw clumsy Life again at her stupid work. For the action taken . . . I had absolutely, and could have, no scrap of use; one had been so perfectly qualified to say in advance: "It's the perfect little workable thing, but she'll strangle it in the cradle, even while she pretends, all so cheeringly, to rock it; wherefore I'll stay her hand while yet there's time."[8]

In like manner the narrator shuns all further intrusions of "clumsy Life."

Even more profoundly like the novelist, he experiences intimacy and passion through the fabric of his imaginative theory alone. The relations between the Brisses and between May Server and Long he can only vicariously construct. Even intimacy with May Server is not finally granted him. Briss has a deeper right to it, for "each [Briss and May] had, by their unprecedented plight, something for the other, some intimacy of unspeakable confidence, that no one else in the world could have for either"(110). Like Rowland speculating on Roderick and Mary Garland, like Isabel wondering about Gilbert Osmond's past, like Maisie trying to understand what goes on among her parents and stepparents, like Strether brooding over Chad's relationship with Jeanne and then with Marie de Vionnet, like Maggie Verver beginning to consider the connection between her husband and her stepmother, like, finally, Henry James writing novels that celebrate intimacy and passion, the narrator has access to these things solely through his own imagination.

Constantly verifying his theory, the narrator makes up for his actual isolation by the unrestricted use of his grasping imagination. He relentlessly analyzes those about him, and their ensuing resentment is suggested as a reason for his ostracism. Throughout the novel he is "fixing," "holding," "grasping" the other major characters. His language is full of hunting and

8. James, *The Art of the Novel*, ed. R. P. Blackmur (New York: Scribner's, 1934), p. 121.

collection imagery; nothing is excluded from his methods of search but "the detective and keyhole"(52). In his constant effort to penetrate beneath appearances, he is explicitly repudiated by Lady John, who tells him to give up trying to be a providence, and by Mrs. Briss, who tells him he's crazy.

The handsome, richly appareled social world takes amiss such a prying gadfly, and he reflects: "I think the imagination, in those halls of art and fortune, was almost inevitably accounted a poor matter; the whole place and its participants abounded so in pleasantness and picture, in all the felicities, for every sense . . . that even the sense most finely poetic, aspiring to extract the moral, could scarce have helped feeling itself treated to something of the snub that affects—when it does affect—the uninvited reporter in whose face a door is closed"(123). The passage is ambivalent, beginning as a defense of the beleaguered moral imagination in a world of social surfaces and closing as rather a critique of the imagination's invasion of others' privacy. "The uninvited reporter" reminds one of the odious Matthias Pardon of *The Bostonians* and perhaps even more of the unnamed narrator—"the publishing scoundrel"—of "The Aspern Papers." Ever since *The American* and *Confidence* James has portrayed such exposure as a temptation to exploit the lives of others by circumscribing their options, their right to develop along their own freely chosen lines.

Moreover, as I argued in my chapter on *The Portrait of a Lady,* the imagination is inevitably exploitative; it shapes the destiny of others according to its own vision. The somewhat dubious "artist-figures" that people James's fiction—of whom Roderick and Rowland, Ralph Touchett and Gilbert Osmond may be taken as earlier examples—are constantly being exposed by the author in their exploitation of others. The novelist, as Jacques Barzun once suggested, is by definition "a spy in enemy country," always exposing and defining his characters, revealing their motives, insidiously from within, for what they are.[9] Thus the narrator (whom I hope by now to have established as analogous to the novelist) knows too much, knows everything, and the internally ravaged May Server appears to him not as a private and unprobed human being but as "such a wasted and dishonoured symbol of [the possibilities of our common nature] as might have put tears in one's eyes"(107).

With this passage in mind one can finally begin to balance the picture and to assess a trait in the narrator seldom attributed to him: for if he coldly exposes, he also lovingly protects. "What was none of one's business might change its name should importunity [exposing May's secret] take the form of utility [protecting her secret]"(74). Here is, I submit, an essential link between James and his narrator: they both seek a relation through which they can give and protect, rather than merely take and expose. The limited point of view, increased stress on surfaces, and a greater ability to suggest depths of significance through judicious details—these are among the formal resources by which such protection is achieved. Partially enlisted in the creation of Isabel Archer's rich and indefinable character, these techniques play a much greater role in James's later fiction; in *The Sacred Fount* they are paramount. For—unlike Barzun's hypothetical novelist—the narrator (and, by implication, James, since he refuses to corroborate or correct the narrator) neither reveals "insidiously from within," nor convinces us that he does indeed "know everything."

In further mitigation of the inevitable "exposure," the narrator has manifest sympathy for the two victims, May and Briss; tears come to his eyes when Briss delivers his wife's mid-

9. "The novel as a genre has been prurient and investigative from the start . . . At first, simple encounters and reversals kept the reader going; lately it has been character and relationships; but it is all one: from Gil Blas to Henry James's 'observer' somebody is always prying." (Jacques Barzun, "Meditations on the Literature of Spying," *American Scholar,* 34 [Spring 1965], 169–170.) One may acknowledge Barzun's point without taking it as far as he does or agreeing that "it is all one."

night message. Nor is this sympathy merely sentimental. He actively aids them in the only ways he can, by bringing them together for mutual comfort and by shielding May from the detection of others. In so doing, he prevaricates and misleads just as the objects of his study do, and he consequently reflects that he has become "as stiff a puzzle to interpretative minds as I had suffered other phenomena to become to my own"(74). Symbolically, through this gesture of commitment to the victims, the novelist enters his creation.

With this basis for the analogy between the narrator and the novelist, we can explore what is too easily discarded by recent critics of the novel—the version of experience posited by the "exquisite theory" of the sacred fount itself:

"One of the pair," I said, "has to pay for the other. What ensues is a miracle, and miracles are expensive. What's a greater one than to have your youth twice over? It's a second wind, another 'go'—which isn't the sort of thing life mostly treats us to. Mrs. Briss had to get her new blood, her extra allowance of time and bloom, somewhere; and from whom could she so conveniently extract them as from Guy himself? She *has*, by an extraordinary feat of legerdemain, extracted them; and he, on his side, to supply her, has had to tap the sacred fount"[24].

Before arguing the importance of the sacred fount theory, one needs to acknowledge the awkwardness of the metaphor. Considered literally or physiologically, the relations posited between the Brisses and between Long and May Server strain credibility when they are not actually embarrassing. One comes too often across such sentences as, "we had suddenly caught Long in the act of presenting his receptacle at the sacred fount"(32), and the physical implications are at the least disconcerting. James himself, with the comic analogy of the turkey dinner(24), seems to recognize the awkwardness of his figure and to mitigate its gravity.

But if the sacred fount is considered less literally, like the ghost in "The Jolly Corner," then its implications can be seen

109

as immense. As a metaphor for the unprotected source of psychic energy, as well as for the precarious seesaw quality in the vital bond between two people, the payments and losses that balance if they do not outweigh gains, James's use of the fount suggests the mutilation, ravage, and unholy gain that are the products, in this novel, of sexual union. It is no accident that those who "gain"—Long and Mrs. Briss—never convince us of the value of their improvement, while those who "lose," those who give themselves to their love—May and Briss—are pathetic, and the object of the narrator's deep commiseration. It is the ravage, not the enrichment, implied by sexual intimacy that James presents most convincingly to the reader, both here and at the conclusion of *The Ambassadors*. If the sacred fount theory fails, as a form for experience, to convey a rich or rewarding vision of human relations, if it always stresses one individual's profit at the expense of his partner rather than a vision of joint fruition or misery, this is because James's art tends toward a vision of mutilation, even of vampirism, rather than more interesting forms of development when it deals with sexual intimacy.

Anyone familiar with Leon Edel's first volume of the James biography will be aware of the possibly personal overtones of "the vampire theory." As Edel indicates, Henry and William seemed to seesaw in cycles of strength and depletion throughout their painful and protracted adolescence. When William was away in Germany, Henry was at his most creative in the States. Conversely, when William began to make intellectual strides, Henry seemed to languish. For example, during William's trip to Brazil in 1866, Henry enjoyed a creative flurry of short stories; on his brother's return, however, Henry's mysterious backache suddenly revived, and his productivity came to a halt. A year later, unwell himself, William left home once again, this time for Germany. Henry's health and spirits immediately and dramatically improved. (For fuller details, see Edel's first volume, especially pages 240–252.) This somewhat sinister phenomenon is writ large in *Watch and Ward* and *The Golden Bowl*, as well as in *The Sacred Fount* and *The Ambassadors*. As critics have noted, it runs as a leitmotif throughout James's short stories, perhaps most blatantly in "De Grey, a Romance," "Longstaff's Marriage," and "Europe." The most striking parallel between the fiction and the biography, however, is the one which Edel has noted between the narrator's reflection on the possible death of Briss through depletion and James's own reflection on the actual death of Minnie Temple through tuberculosis:

She [Mrs. Briss] would have loved his youth, and have made it her own, in death as in life, and he would have quitted the world, in truth, only the more effectually to leave it to her[80].

It's almost as if she had passed away—as far as I am concerned—from having served her purpose, that of standing well within the world, inviting and inviting me onward by all the bright intensity of her example.[10]

As an imaginative form for experience, the metaphor of the sacred fount has implications that are central to my study of James, and one might begin by noticing that the real cost of romantic miracles is at the heart of *Roderick Hudson, The Portrait of a Lady,* and *The Ambassadors.* The miracle consists of an unprecedented transformation, an ideal development of the self beyond any realistic expectations. In *The Portrait of a Lady* the imagery of free expansion corresponds to this desire on Isabel's part for untrammeled self-fulfillment; as in *Roderick Hudson,* the aspiration is expressed through fairy-tale and romance motifs. But the fairy tale of Roderick's limitless self-fulfillment ends in his own death; and as "the real"—"the things we cannot possibly *not* know"—makes its presence increasingly felt, Rowland is reduced from fairy godfather to

10. Excerpt from a letter to William, quoted in Leon Edel, *Henry James: The Untried Years* (Philadelphia: J. B. Lippincott, 1953), p. 326.

scapegoat. Similarly Isabel's romantic dreams of self-development culminate in a cul-de-sac: "She had taken all the first steps in the purest of confidence, and then she had suddenly found the infinite vista of a multiplied life to be a dark, narrow alley with a dead wall at the end"(II,189). In *The Ambassadors,* as I shall stress later, the expense of the miracle moves us more, perhaps, than the miracle itself, and *The Sacred Fount* passage serves as an eloquent gloss on Chad's transformation, Marie de Vionnet's payment for it, and Strether's curious "second wind."

The form of experience implied by the narrator's theory, then, cannot be cavalierly discarded as symptomatic only of his disordered mind. In its version of sexual intimacy, it casts light on James's treatment of human relationships throughout his fiction. And in its articulation of the extremes of the romantic (miracles) and the real (their cost), of self-development and self-sacrifice, as well as in its projection of the inevitable interaction of these, it serves as a synoptic form for the kinds of experience I have been looking at throughout the novels.

Founded upon intimacy,[11] as in *What Maisie Knew,* this experience, from which the narrator, like Maisie, is fundamentally excluded, is both appalling and sublime. Appalling in the profit that one lover extracts from the other; sublime in the self-sacrifice the other lover makes to meet this incessant demand. I would suggest that this unholy union of exploitation and abnegation, though often only latent, lies near the center of James's fictive attitude toward sexual relations and that the ambiguous attitude toward human intimacy—the mixture of fear and approval—that I explored in *The Portrait of a Lady* corresponds to the fusion of the appalling and the sublime embodied in the sacred fount relationship.

To demonstrate the ravage caused by passion, one goes unhesitatingly to the narrator's view of the exploited May Server:

11. " 'And the relation—to do that sort of thing—must be necessarily so awfully intimate.' *'Intimissima'* "(28).

"I saw as I had never seen before what consuming passion can make of the marked mortal on whom, with fixed beak and claws, it has settled as on a prey. She reminded me of a sponge wrung dry and with fine pores agape. Voided and scraped of everything, her shell was merely crushable. So it was brought home to me that the victim could be abased, and so it disengaged itself from these things that the abasement could be conscious"(106–107).

If one searches *The Sacred Fount* for other corroborative passages of the exposure of the cost of passion, one finds nothing remotely like this one. That is, a basic postulate of the narrator's theory is that the lovers *protect* each other, and what one discovers throughout the novel is a maddening proliferation of screens (or, more maddening yet, of possible screens). Therefore, when Lady John and the narrator figuratively bump heads together in looking at the momentary conjunction of Long and Mrs. Briss, the narrator is incensed at Lady John's presumably vulgar induction that the observed couple are having an affair: "It was better verily not to have touched them [Long and Mrs. Briss] . . . than to have taken them up, with knowing gestures, only to do so little with them"(145).

The passage is charged with implications. Lady John may indeed be vulgarly right, for the novel presents a powerful unacknowledged case for Mrs. Briss and Long being lovers. In addition, this is the language of Henry James in the Prefaces, insisting upon the maximum exhaustion of his materials. Unlike Lady John's facile induction, the narrator's theory postulates privacy, not exposure. As he sees it, the two "victors" are coming together, not the two lovers, since the primary strategy of the lovers is to conceal their passion. Each appears with other possible lovers, he decides, only to subvert analysis.

Relying always upon the unseen, the narrator is exasperatingly pleased with the least suspicion of concealment, for he is unlimited in his freedom to "interpret" recalcitrant appearances so as to make them consonant with the dissimilar reality he imagines beneath them. He is not bound by the ostensible import of appearances, since anything could be a screen. On the other hand, he expressly forbids himself to base his judgments upon anything *but* appearances; he will hear no confessions.

The larger uncertainties of the novel, and indeed the tantalizing, if obsessive, concern in James's later work with the meaning behind the form (in both conversation and appearances) can be partly traced to this solicitude for his characters' privacy: "It could *not* but be exciting to talk, as we talked, on the basis of those suppressed processes and unavowed references which made the meaning of our meeting so different from its form"(212). Such conversations, suggesting everything but revealing nothing, are indeed "exciting," and they are a hallmark of the late style. Indeed, one might ask, waiving value questions for the moment, is not *The Sacred Fount* a perfect example of the novel that explores without defining, that exposes without deadening, that begins as a detective story but ends—through ambiguity—in privacy?

What generalizations, finally, can be made about *The Sacred Fount* without denying its essential ambiguity? Primarily it presents a vision of the artist, and I suggest this despite all the qualifications registered against the narrator. Critics have carefully noted his isolation from the other characters, his lack of conclusive proof, his possible misinterpretation of appearances, his cold exposure and sacrifice of others to his theory, his annoying, often comic, habit of meddling into others' affairs; critics have noticed these indications of James's ironic stance and, therefore, dismissed all analogies to the novelist himself. What they seem to have disregarded is that the isolation and the lack of "experiential" proof are in part self-imposed, that the absence of certitude is many times acknowledged, and that the coldness is balanced by sympathy, the exploitation by protection, the exposure by secrecy. Beyond this,

what has been insufficiently recognized—in connection with
The Sacred Fount—is that the artistic enterprise comes under
an exacting scrutiny throughout James's work and that he not
only examined critically the moral quality of his vocation, but
he also created a fictive world whose characteristic activity
is analogous to his own creative behavior. An ambiguous and
critically presented narrator need not establish the novelist's
distance so much as his confession of complicity.

This is surely not to argue that the narrator and James are
analogous in all particulars. Rather, the liabilities of James's
calling are dramatized and exaggerated, often comically, in
his rendering of the narrator, but the justification of the narrator's enterprise, though only shadowy, is recurrently hinted
at throughout the novel; and this flickering approval has caused
confusion among critics who simply "dismiss" him.

The narrator must be seen as both exploitative and protective. Coming on May Server, he reflects upon his "extraordinary tenderness" for her, while in the same paragraph,
as he moves in, he feels "almost as noiseless and guarded as
if I were trapping a bird or stalking a fawn"(102). Likewise,
when poor depleted Briss delivers the message from his wife,
the strongly sympathetic narrator perceives that Briss has been
freshly drained ("he had never been so much poor Briss as
at this moment"), and then reflects: "his being there . . . re-
newed my sources and replenished my current—spoke all, in
short, for my gain"(176). The image of the enriched current
is clearly akin to the sacred fount image itself, for, as many
have noticed, the narrator is a kind of vampire, draining others
in the service of his theory.

At the same time, he is drained by the others, for May
Server's protection and Mrs. Briss's consciousness are both gifts
of his. In the final interview with Mrs. Briss, he is being relentlessly depleted, and he knows quite well that, as to her
dazzlingly appearing only twenty-five years old, he will somehow have to pay for it(188). Though isolated from the sexual

intimacy posited by the sacred fount theory, he yet enacts—in his exploitative-sacrificial relationship with the other characters, in his alternately draining or being drained by them—what might be called an aesthetic version of the same theory.

With these mixed characteristics in mind, one might explore some of the possible meanings implicit in that equivocal concluding interview. At the simplest level the scene could suggest the inevitable confrontation of art with life: "she waited as if it were a question of dashing her head at a wall. Then, at last, she charged. 'It's nonsense. I've nothing to tell you. I feel there's nothing in it and I've given it up' "(195). Pictured as a bull, Mrs. Briss charges and brings crumbling down the narrator's "palace of thought," his "house of cards." Long is unchanged; so is May. The narrator is crazy. His theory is lovely and rich but simply unsupported by the facts.[12]

Mrs. Briss may vanquish him through the fragility of his method without establishing her own version of things. She may indeed, as his theory posits, have sided with Long and be protecting her own victim from the narrator's inquiry. Or else, and this is strongly suggested, her real intimacy may be with Long, not with Briss at all, and she wants to get rid of the narrator before he finds her out. His obsession with the theory may thus have prevented the narrator from seeing what is under his nose, just as Dr. Sloper's intransigent theory of his daughter's stupidity prevents him from perceiving her painful development into maturity in *Washington Square*.

The experience posited by the narrator's theory is in any case far from successfully contradicted. Mrs. Briss is shown throughout the last fifty pages as drawing her strength not

12. Precisely analogous to Mrs. Briss's "nonrecognition" is Sarah Pocock's inability (or refusal) to see any changes whatsoever in Chad (except the ones she had feared). The narrator's argument, like Strether's "defense," is rendered impotent in the face of impercipience ("for she need, obviously, only decline to take one of my counters to deprive it of all value as coin"[245]).

only from Briss—in their marital intimacy he "confessed" all—but also from the narrator. As she gains power, he weakens, until she has left him as old as Briss: "I didn't after all—it appeared part of my smash—know the weight of her husband's years, but I knew the weight of my own. They might have been a thousand, and nothing but the sense of them would in a moment, I saw, be left me" (248). Drinking at her husband's fount and at the narrator's—for *he* cannot disavow her stunning transformation, even though she disavow Long's—Mrs. Briss proves the theory by vanquishing its proponent.

She has drawn consciousness from him as a character draws it from the novelist-creator, and, as she grows progressively "free," so her motives become indecipherable. She becomes less and less a mere abstract symbol and more and more the embodiment of a vivid tone. She thus represents, one may argue, an unanswerable challenge to the narrator's authority, just as, by extension, *The Sacred Fount* may be seen as James's confession of the precarious authority, the questionable bases, of his own art.

All of these are possible meanings; the text is pregnant with ambiguities that multiply the more one studies them. Through his intent to protect and suggest, rather than to define, James has created a tour de force, a novel in which virtually nothing is authoritatively known, and in which the imagination of both narrator and reader is almost intolerably exercised. In this way alone the novel can confess to its double failure as an art form: its failure either fully to protect or fully to establish the relations with which it is concerned. In this way alone, likewise, it achieves its peculiar double success: "For all its vividness, it [the form of the novel] shields, rather than brutally exposes, the realities it presents (even Mrs. Briss's actual motives)'. And for all its uncertainty, the form successfully presents a range of experience which it will not and cannot encounter directly; it *intimates* the realities which his [the narrator's] penetrating scrutiny has made vividly present to himself and brought within the reader's presence."[13]

By limiting himself to an isolated narrator and by focusing entirely on that narrator's unsuccessful quest for knowledge, James places greater stress upon the discrepancy between appearance and reality than he does in any other of his works. Only in "The Turn of the Screw" and "In the Cage" is there a comparable exploration; yet one must qualify the analogy between the governess and the narrator of the *Fount*. Objective knowledge is equally unascertainable in her story, but the cumulated horrors that develop under her aegis—Miles dies, and something terrible happens to Flora—place a correspondingly greater strain upon her "point of view." After all, though he is at times insufferable, the narrator of the *Fount* does not demonstrably injure anyone else. In this sense he resembles more the unnamed telegraphist of "In the Cage": both are imaginative, surrounded by the social world, and essentially isolated from it. The only profound experience either ever undergoes comes through the medium of the vicarious imagination, and it is from this vantage point that each story is projected.

The Sacred Fount, alone among James's novels, is a full-length demonstration of the imagination serving as the locus of all experience: "It would have been almost as embarrassing to have to tell them how little experience I had had in fact as to have had to tell them how much I had had in fancy" (80). The narrator's experience is inevitably cerebral, just as his feeling remains private. With every character he interrogates, he engages in a ritual of exploitation or protection, always retaining immaculate his own psychic isolation. Nothing is fully shared. Intimacy and passion obsess his mind but fail to characterize any of his own relationships; at the novel's conclusion he is "smashed," distraught, in retreat.

13. Holland, *Expense of Vision,* p. 210. For a fuller indication of the range of these possible "realities," see pp. 202–203.

And yet there is a kind of attenuated intimacy in the novel, that between reader and narrator. It could be called a "literary" intimacy, the product both of his ingenuously confiding in us alone and of his process of intimating rather than formally or baldly stating his conclusions. He shares information with us without ever communicating it openly, as though we were friends who, of course, "understand" his elusive thoughts without making him dot the "i's" and cross the "t's." His cryptic imaginative leaps are responded to by our own in the absence of proof or complete disclosure. And proof must remain absent because the narrator restricts himself entirely to appearances, effecting a sort of protection for the reality beneath them; it is a reality that must be imaginatively inferred, can never be revealed. The decorum that results is characteristic of all of James's later fiction. Surfaces are scrupulously respected. What lies beneath them is ascertainable, if at all, through the probing imagination of a solitary individual in the novel or a reader outside of it.

Characters, then, are free to develop their own attributes; no one goes behind authoritatively and tells us what to think. In this way, James relates to his characters by allowing them to become—through the protective freedom he bestows upon them—complexly living people rather than—through the exposure of final analysis—dead, dishonored symbols. Such freedom, I believe, confusedly "explains" the unreliable narration in *The Sacred Fount*, "explains" Mrs. Briss's weird and inscrutable victory over the narrator, "explains" the reader's inability to "fix" exactly what happened and, consequently, exactly who everyone is. Protection, even though it infuriates the reader, is being achieved, and the novelist, through his narrator, has succeeded in imagining a story without fully identifying the characters who make it up.

It is a technical success, however, whose value depends greatly on what the novelist is able to do with it. In Proust's major work and in Faulkner's finest novels—*The Sound and the Fury* and *Absalom, Absalom!*—James's experiments with unreliable narration and the romance of subjective perception are magnificently adapted and vindicated. But in *The Sacred Fount,* one finally says to oneself, precious little else is going on; the story of a story that fails to become clear makes, in the absence of other interests, a thin literary diet. Passion and intimacy—the subjects of the obsession—are absent from the novel in all but the most attenuated, cerebral forms. In fact, passion and intimacy are so muffled that the reader begins to wonder if the distance of reverent protection is not also the distance of abhorrence and repulsion, if the narrator's inexperience of these things is also the novelist's, and if the imagination is the only prism through which he can come at them, both by default and by design. Is the obsessive imagination of passionate experience a substitute, through fear, for the experience itself?

The vision of life posited by the sacred fount theory, if taken seriously, is a fearful one, and there is every reason to believe that James was consciously experimenting with it. The gain and loss implied by its version of passion and intimacy—the profit and the cost of a close personal relationship—were soon to reappear in Chad and in Marie de Vionnet. And the gain and loss that come from merely imagining rather than undergoing such experience, from being repelled by its violence and thus substituting the vision of intimacy for intimacy itself—this only too clearly continued to fascinate James. If he painted a partial portrait of himself and his artistic stance toward experience in the narrator of *The Sacred Fount,* within the next year he was to create his two most haunting figures of the imagined as opposed to the realized life: John Marcher in "The Beast in the Jungle" and Lambert Strether in *The Ambassadors.*

V Strether's Curious "Second Wind": Imagination and Experience in *The Ambassadors*

*"One of the pair," I said, "has to pay for the other. What
ensues is a miracle, and miracles are expensive. What's a greater
one than to have your youth twice over? It's a second wind, another 'go'—which isn't the sort of thing life mostly treats us to."*
The Sacred Fount

*What happened all the while, I conceive, was that I imagined
things . . . wholly other than as they were, and so carried on
in the midst of the actual ones an existence that somehow
floated and saved me even while cutting me off from any degree
of direct performance, in fact from any degree of direct participation, at all.*
Henry James, Autobiography

Perception is not whimsical, but fatal.
Emerson, "Self-Reliance"

UNLIKE *The Sacred Fount*, *The Ambassadors* fully merits the
critical attention it has received. Whether it be his best novel
or, as Warner Berthoff puts it, "only his most perfectly charming," it has elicited brilliant commentary from Percy Lubbock
in 1921 to Sallie Sears in 1968. Their work, as well as that
of Oscar Cargill, Laurence Holland, Christof Wegelin, Robert
Garis, Tony Tanner, and Richard Poirier, has proved particu-

larly helpful, but the book remains inexhaustible. The pages that follow are not so much a challenge to the above critics as a fleshed-out reading of the particular drama—located among the many dramas indicated by others—that *The Ambassadors* seems most interestingly to embody: the fundamental relation between a character's imagination, the experience he seeks to interpret, and the experience he finally undergoes.[1]

As observer-actor, Strether represents the mature development of a kind of character James first seriously sketched in Rowland Mallet. The earlier character, possessed of a "moral and aesthetic curiosity" (*Roderick Hudson*, 16), ambiguously connected with the drama of a younger man toward whom he is expected to act as a moral guardian of sorts, and finally stranded on his return to America, is an unmistakable precursor of Strether. And we can measure a certain direction of James's development by the difference in our response to the two men.

In the early novel James seems undecided as to his primary subject, vacillating in emphasis between Roderick's adventures and Rowland's perception of them. As I suggested in my first

1. Percy Lubbock, *The Craft of Fiction* (New York: Scribner's, 1921), pp. 145–149, 156–171; Sallie Sears, *The Negative Imagination: Form and Perception in the Novels of Henry James* (Ithaca, N.Y.: Cornell University Press, 1968), pp. 99–151; Oscar Cargill, *The Novels of Henry James* (New York: Macmillan, 1961), pp. 303–337; Laurence Holland, *The Expense of Vision: Essays on the Craft of Henry James* (Princeton, N.J.: Princeton University Press, 1964), pp. 229–282; Christof Wegelin, *The Image of Europe in Henry James* (Dallas, Tex.: Southern Methodist University Press, 1958), pp. 88–105; Robert E. Garis, "The Two Lambert Strethers: A New Reading of *The Ambassadors*," *Modern Fiction Studies*, 7 (Winter 1961–62), 305–316; Tony Tanner, "The Watcher from the Balcony: Henry James's *The Ambassadors*," *Critical Quarterly*, 8 (Spring 1966), 35–52; Richard Poirier, *A World Elsewhere* (New York: Oxford University Press, 1966), pp. 124–143. Other critics from whom I have benefited include Frederick Crews, *The Tragedy of Manners: Moral Drama in the Later Novels of Henry James* (New Haven, Conn.: Yale University Press, 1957), pp. 30–56; F. O. Matthiessen, *Henry James: The Major Phase* (New York: Oxford University Press, 1944), pp. 18–41; Stephen Spender, *The Destructive Element* (London: Jonathan Cape, 1935), pp. 75–83; and Ian Watt, "The First Paragraph of *The Ambassadors*: An Explication," in *The Ambassadors*, ed. S. P. Rosenbaum (New York: W. W. Norton, 1964), pp. 465–484.

chapter, this dilemma serves as a turning point in the development of James's characteristic view of experience. The Roderick figure continues in Newman, in the early Isabel, in Basil Ransom, in Paul Muniment, and in Chad. But the figure who means most for James's development, and who leads to Ralph Touchett and to the Isabel of Book II, to Hyacinth, Fleda Vetch, Maisie, Nanda, the narrator of *The Sacred Fount,* Strether, Milly, and Maggie, is surely the sensitive and observant, the passive and imaginative Rowland Mallet.[2]

In *The Ambassadors* the main subject—Strether—is developed with a massive fullness unmatched elsewhere in James's fiction. Every conversation, every observed, imagined, or remembered relationship has an interest both in itself and as it bears on Strether's fate. Although the consciousness of Rowland Mallet was the point of view for telling Roderick's story in the earlier novel, Rowland himself remained at times only vaguely implicated in the sculptor's life, and the comparative thinness of *Roderick Hudson* derives from James's failure to establish vividly either the drama or Roderick's adventures or the intensity of Rowland's relation to them.

In his next important novels James seems to have combined (in Christopher Newman and in Isabel Archer) the roles of actor and observer that were fragmented in *Roderick Hudson;* Isabel looms as large in her novel as Strether does in his. But, although one sees mainly from her perspective, the contours of her mind and the precise nature of her emotional responses are rarely so intimately known as Strether's are. Isabel remains a magnificent creation but often inscrutable, rendered somehow from the outside; Strether, despite James's poised, complex stance toward him, is presented more tenderly and more nearly from within.

This is a loosely expressed point, but one with important

2. This chapter was originally written before I came across Tony Tanner's essay on *The Ambassadors,* in which he sees the connection between Rowland and Strether but lacks space to develop it.

ramifications. Because we are relatively farther from Isabel's mind than from Strether's, and because the world she encounters is seen by us as immediately other than the way she sees it, we develop a more detached and critical attitude toward her romance. In other words, by not giving us, in *The Ambassadors,* a scene, like the early, clarifying one between Gilbert Osmond and Madame Merle, by refracting everything through Strether's consciousness, James prevents us from incisively "placing" Strether's errors as we can place Isabel's. Consequently, Strether's imagination plays a broader and more sympathetic role than Isabel's in shaping the reader's response. This change in emphasis has important implications: first, it accounts for the richly embroidered, playful prose of *The Ambassadors;* more important, however, it underlies our final feeling that, while Isabel has been cheated, Strether *has* somehow had his experience. By keeping us gently critical of Isabel's imagination and then concluding her experience with loss and disillusionment, James makes us respond to the ending of *The Portrait of a Lady* as tragic.

But the conclusion of *The Ambassadors* occasions in us no such somber response. Unlike Isabel, Strether has largely and consciously limited his goal to the realm of the imagination alone: when other realms fail and Strether departs with nothing else, he has at least (or supremely) had his imaginative adventure. Placed within his mind, we feel no tragic loss; we have, in a sense, undergone his experience with him, an experience impaired but not, like Isabel's, bitterly mocked by the losses and renunciations with which the novel ends. These differences should become clearer in my analysis of *The Ambassadors.*

Among the protagonists who precede Strether, Maisie and the narrator of *The Sacred Fount,* do not "act," as Isabel does, on the grand scale. Like Rowland and Ralph Touchett, they are primarily engaged in seeing, but the emphasis in their stories shifts increasingly from what they see to how they see.

Moreover, they become central rather than peripheral characters. To oversimplify, one might say that *The Sacred Fount* is comparable to *Roderick Hudson* without Roderick or to *The Portrait of a Lady* projected from Ralph Touchett's point of view, without the solid presence of Isabel Archer and her well-defined drama. In his quest for perception, Strether of course resembles Maisie and the narrator of *The Sacred Fount*. But *The Ambassadors*—unlike the two shorter novels that precede it and harking back to the novels of the eighties—reasserts a major stress on the world being perceived. Put more concretely, the physical and human worlds of Paris, of Chad and Madame de Vionnet, are rendered by James as something real, something important in their own right, not primarily as an index to Strether's mind. And yet the triumph of the novel is that Strether's mind is portrayed, through its contact with these worlds, with a more impressive delicacy and intensity than James achieves in the creation of either Maisie or the narrator of the *Fount*.

Strether embodies characteristics and concerns that have been common to James's earlier heroes from Rowland to the narrator of *The Sacred Fount*. Moreover, in the spectrum of life confronted by Strether, *The Ambassadors* presents a synthesis of the two major kinds of experience that this study has been exploring. To encounter the world of European civilization, in *Roderick Hudson* and in *The Portrait of a Lady*, is one of the deepest desires of the protagonist; for Isabel Archer, it is paramount. *What Maisie Knew* and *The Sacred Fount* project, however, a range of experience both narrower and, in a sense, more basic. Passive and psychically isolated, Maisie and the narrator cannot afford the "luxury" of Isabel's adventures. Up to their necks in an epistemological morass, they are not concerned with the refinement that comes from an encounter with the "great world." Rather, they struggle at the elementary level of meaning itself; their attempt is simply to make some sense of the world of passion and intimacy that

surrounds them. In *The Ambassadors,* through Strether's adventure, as later in *The Golden Bowl,* the odyssey into European civilization and the encounter with sexual intimacy merge
into a comprehensive rendering of the Jamesian vision of
human experience.

Finally, because of his age, his past, his temperament, and
his peculiar errand, Strether's experience of the European
world comes to him largely as shaped by his imagination. To
examine his drama in Paris is to explore the interplay between
the energies of one of James's most imaginative heroes and
the outside world of the largest, most typical experience. As
justification for such a detailed analysis of this novel, I suggest
that the shape of Strether's drama is indeed the figure in the
carpet of James's work, the major trope with which this study
has been concerned.

Live all you can, it's a mistake not to. It doesn't so much matter
what you do in particular, so long as you have your life. If you
haven't had that what *have* you had?

That, you see, is my only logic. Not, out of the whole affair,
to have got anything for myself.[3]

Between these two speeches—each pointing to an opposite
extreme—one can locate Strether's approach toward experience. Overwhelmed by the magnificent pageant in Gloriani's
garden, Strether recalls the failed occasions and accumulated
mediocrity of his own life, and he passionately urges little
Bilham not to make the same mistake. Although couched in
deterministic phrases (not quoted here) that acknowledge that
it is too late for himself, Strether's outburst is a paean to free-

3. James, *The Ambassadors* (New York: Scribner's, 1909),I,217;
II,326. Subsequent quotations from *The Ambassadors* refer to this edition
(Volumes XXI and XXII of the New York Ed.); hereafter, all page
references will be included within the text, parenthetically, after the
quotation.

dom and self-development, an exhortation to live life to the fullest. It contrasts vividly with the reflective, fastidious tone of the later speech in which Strether justifies self-denial as the only possible conclusion to his experience. This chapter attempts to relate these contradictory speeches: to qualify the first one and, as regards the second, to suggest what, after all, Strether does get for himself "out of the whole affair."

That he was prepared to be vague to Waymarsh about the hour of the ship's touching, and that he both wanted extremely to see him and enjoyed extremely the duration of delay—these things, it is to be conceived, were early signs in him that his relation to his actual errand might prove none of the simplest. He was burdened, poor Strether—it had better be confessed at the outset—with the oddity of a double consciousness. There was detachment in his zeal and curiosity in his indifference[I,5].

Some light on Strether's ambiguous position is cast by this passage, which occurs on the third page of the narrative and caps a series of uneasy meditations that began with the novel's opening phrase: "Strether's first question." Strether is constantly (and delightfully) asking questions and having misgivings throughout his adventure. The uneasiness derives from his "oddity of a double consciousness," and, in his conflicting desires to experience Europe and to remain true to his moral categories, he exhibits a duality that echoes Isabel Archer's "mixture of curiosity and fastidiousness, of vivacity and indifference" (*Portrait*,I,69).

On the one hand, Strether has been assigned the specific task of bringing Chad back to the fold, and any enjoyment in the interim is liable to undermine his precarious authority. Thus his trip to Europe can be seen as an uncomfortable, sacrificial ordeal undergone for Mrs. Newsome; and Maria Gostrey, seeing it at first in these terms, remarks: "You'd do at any rate this [go to Europe for Mrs. Newsome and Sarah], and the 'anything' they'd do is represented by their *making* you do it"(I,57). Of course Strether knows (and this is what makes him uneasy) that they are not "making" him do anything, that, furtively and for a long time, he has yearned to return to Europe and redeem his "promise" made thirty years ago. When Maria concludes that he is not "enjoying it" so much as he ought, she is unaware of the complexity of motives and characteristics in Strether that make him capable of enjoying Europe less than he wants to and more than he thinks he ought to.

The commitment to Woollett is a complex one, composed of admiration and gratitude toward Mrs. Newsome—she is, after all, the only person who has acted toward him in a generous way since the death of his own family—but composed also of material promises, of a future full of peace and security for his old age. Underlying both of these aspects of the Woollett commitment are certain buried moral premises and attitudes toward experience that become resurrected and transformed during the course of his adventure in Paris.

Opposing the commitment to Mrs. Newsome, on the other hand, is a concealed but profound desire to make the most of his European experience. Strether has always been vaguely aware of his personal failure, and the return to Paris makes this awareness throb: "The special spring that had constantly played for him the day before was the recognition—frequent enough to surprise him—of the promises to himself that he had after his other visit never kept"(I,85). Moreover, the "consciousness of personal freedom as he hadn't known for years"(I,4) implies that Mrs. Newsome and the marriage that awaits his return home are already viewed with mixed feelings. Freedom and experience—the dream of a certain fulfillment—are felt by Strether in Paris rather than anticipated as rewards attending his homecoming: it both surprises and embarrasses him to note how much his being in Paris figures for him as an escape. The betrayal of his youthful promises made years ago in Paris is further compounded by a later "betrayal" of his own son; through unrestrained grief for his

128

wife's untimely death, Strether grew estranged from his son, and the latter's death has left Strether scarred with feelings of guilt.

The sense of personal failure, the ambiguous feeling toward his Woollett future, and the guilt incurred from "betraying" his own son render him especially vulnerable to Chad's Parisian drama. Adoption of Chad's point of view will symbolically redeem Strether's earlier failure to profit by Paris; to befriend Chad is, again symbolically, to atone for his failure toward his dead son. These reasons for Strether's susceptibility are sufficient to account for his squirming throughout the novel; anchored in his cultural inheritance and his own past, they act as a background for his European adventure. What brings them into play and gives unique shape to Strether's experience in Paris, what quickens both his enjoyment and his self-criticism, is his faculty of appreciation, his ripening imagination.

Strether embarks for Europe with what may be called a Woollett imagination; he and the town's moral emblem—Mrs. Newsome—see Chad the same way. They both have imagined "horrors," and he is consequently amazed by Maria Gostrey's exclamation, "She may be charming—his life!"

"Charming?"—Strether stared before him. "She's base, venal—out of the streets."

"I see. And *he*—?"

"Chad, wretched boy?"

"Of what type and temper is he?" she went on as Strether had lapsed.

"Well—the obstinate." It was as if for a moment he had been going to say more and had then controlled himself.

That was scarce what she wished. "Do you like him?"

This time he was prompt. "No. How *can* I?"

"Do you mean because of your being so saddled with him?"

"I'm thinking of his mother," said Strether after a moment. "He has darkened her admirable life." He spoke with austerity [I,55].

"Intensity with ignorance" (II,242), Maria's later phrase for Mrs. Newsome's imagination, aptly describes Strether's own in this scene. Trying to elicit a concrete description of the "problem," Maria succeeds in drawing from Strether only abstract phrases of moral condemnation. His codified point of view stymies the conversation and blocks the passage of any information other than his own righteous disapproval. Stung by what he can only consider the perversity of Maria's questions, Strether is unable detachedly to consider Chad as a complex human being ("No. How *can* I?"), and the consequent impoverishment of his perceptions is expressed by the clichés that creep into his conversation: "She's base, venal—out of the streets"; "Chad, wretched boy"; "He has darkened her admirable life."[4] These are closed-minded, dogmatic judgments, just the reverse of those marvelous exploratory conversations found elsewhere in James, which are punctuated by question marks and seek new information, rather than doctrinally elaborating old positions. Warned by his tone, Maria Gostrey cannot enlighten him. She has no choice but hypocrisy ("I see"), and Strether is saved from a fate of "splendid" isolation—like Waymarsh's—only through his ability to develop beyond this position.

The Woollett imagination in Strether expresses itself not only through clichés but also through the limited meanings he is able to attach to certain phrases: " '*Now* don't you see,' she [Maria] went on, 'why the boy doesn't come home? He's drowning his shame.' 'His shame? [Strether replies] What shame?' " (I,62). The interchange rises effortlessly to a contrast between Puritan New England and aesthetic Paris. Maria

---

4. Increasingly aware of the crude inadequacy and cliché nature of his moral categories—"Excuse me, but I must really . . . know where I am. Is she bad?"—Strether painfully seeks the right phrase and wades yet deeper into the morass: "Is her life without reproach?" Chad artfully answers Strether with his own categories and ends with a hint of the antidote for their deficiency: "Absolutely without reproach. A beautiful life. *Allez donc voir!*" (I,239).

posits the dubiously acquired Newsome fortune as the "shame" from which the finer-grained Chad is fleeing; while to Strether's imagination how one makes money is virtually outside moral categories, the obviously outrageous shame in the affair being Chad's corruption by a "base, venal" woman.

The richest example of an untutored imagination revealed through ignorance of what words may mean occurs in a colloquy with little Bilham: " 'He wants to be free. He isn't used, you see,' the young man explained in his lucid way, 'to being so good.' Strether hesitated. 'Then I may take it from you that he *is* good?' His companion matched his pause, but making it up with a quiet fulness. '*Do* take it from me.' " Strether then persists, "Why isn't he free if he's good?" to which, looking him "full in the face," little Bilham finally replies, "Because it's a virtuous attachment"(I,178–180).

Strether's one-sided application of moral terms to an illicit sexual union leads him quite awry. If Chad is "good," he reasons, he must then be "free" and cannot be sexually involved. In little Bilham's view, however, freedom is incommensurate with such goodness, and this darker equation, while unknown to Strether, serves the reader as a qualification of the famous outburst in Gloriani's garden, for it unobtrusively prefigures the losses and renunciations—the "cost" of being "good"—with which the novel closes. Strether, however, is unaware of these complications; at this point "a virtuous attachment" is for his imagination, if not for little Bilham's, a simplifying rubric.

But once he has seen Chad, everything begins to alter, and the second "phase" of the journey of Strether's imagination commences with his appreciating to the full Chad's marvelous transformation: "Chad's case—whatever else of minor interest it might yield—was first and foremost a miracle almost monstrous. It was the alteration of the entire man, and was so signal an instance that nothing else, for the intelligent observer, could—*could* it?—signify"(I,167). The extreme phrasing—"miracle almost monstrous," "entire man," "nothing else," "*could* it?"—conveys the wonder and possible excess of Strether's reaction. Moored for years to Woollett's horizons, his liberated imagination has, in the phrase used for Isabel Archer, "jumped out of the window." After a lifetime of inertia and mediocrity, now furtively seeking in Europe something he began thirty years before but failed to make good on, Strether is quick to see in Chad transcendent development, a man made over. It is a case of fatal perception; Strether *has* glimpsed something extraordinary, and later qualifications can only reduce his estimate of Chad without marring the beauty of his vision. The image of successful change and the apparent realization of his long-abandoned European ideal touch his own private desires too nearly to be relinquished. Chad moves Strether most deeply not as a substitute son but as the living embodiment of the youth he now realizes he never remotely had.

This growing fascination with youth lends a vivid allure to the silhouetted figure of little Bilham on the balcony:

He was young too then, the gentleman up there—he was very young . . . there was youth in the surrender to the balcony, there was youth for Strether at this moment in everything but his own business; and Chad's thus pronounced association with youth had given the next instant an extraordinary quick lift to the issue. The balcony, the distinguished front, testified suddenly, for Strether's fancy, to something that was up and up; they placed the whole case materially, and as by an admirable image, on a level that he found himself at the end of another moment rejoicing to think he might reach . . . It came to pass before he moved that Waymarsh, and Waymarsh alone . . . struck him as the present alternative to the young man in the balcony. When he did move it was fairly to escape that alternative[I,97–99].

The passage exhibits the power of Strether's "fancy" to create a symbolic, "admirable image" from a natural situation, and Strether's climbing to the height of that balcony, like his later climbing those same four stories "for Chad's life" (II,306), translates his imaginative vision into active experience, into gestures of personal commitment. As with Isabel, however, the gesture of self-assertion is also an "escape" from "alternatives" suddenly seen as intolerable.

In Gloriani's garden, where Parisian life is most before him, Strether understandably links the sculptor's charm with Chad's unfailing ease and, through that connection, with his own yearning: "Chad . . . was a kind of link for hopeless fancy, an implication of possibilities—oh if everything had been different!"(I,198). At the end of the party the connection through memory between his abortive youth and Chad's achievement is complete: " 'Oh Chad!'—it was that rare youth he should have enjoyed being 'like' "(I,220). The implications of this connection are writ large in Strether's behavior in Paris and will be explored later. I am concerned here with the imaginative release it occasions in Strether, as is indicated in the following outburst to Maria Gostrey:

I don't get drunk; I don't pursue the ladies; I don't spend money; I don't even write sonnets. But nevertheless I'm making up late for what I didn't have early . . . It amuses me more than anything that has happened to me in all my life. They may say what they like—it's my surrender, it's my tribute, to youth. One puts that in where one can—it has to come in somewhere, if only out of the lives, the conditions, the feelings of other persons. Chad gives me the sense of it, for all his grey hairs . . . and *she* does the same, for all her marriageable daughter, her separated husband, her agitated history. Though they're young enough, my pair, I don't say they're . . . their *own* absolutely prime adolescence; for that has nothing to do with it. The point is that they're mine. Yes, they're my youth; since somehow at the right time nothing else ever was[II,50–51].

Madame de Vionnet, too, is part of his youth, and if his imaginative vision of Chad is shaped by the current of memory, what his imagination makes of her is even more strikingly a creation of his dormant ideals and desires. As with his encounter with Chad at the theater, Strether's first impression of Madame de Vionnet is too "massive" to be related in the present tense alone. "He was to feel"(I,210), "our friend was to go over it afterwards again and again"(I,135)—these fusions of the past and future tenses indicate how the sheer weight of Strether's impressions and the lavish care he devotes to them transcend the moment when they are made. While the vision of Chad summoned the memory of Strether's own past, Madame de Vionnet gradually comes symbolically to bridge for him an even greater number of years, to represent the historic beauty and continuity of French civilization.

His first impression, which a little disappoints his Woollett curiosity about the exotic, is of her "common humanity"(I,213); and he is puzzled that a woman so like his female acquaintances might possibly be Chad's lover. His imagination begins to embroider her traits, however, as he sees in her dignified apartment a hint of the ancient Paris, "some glory, some prosperity of the First Empire, some Napoleonic glamour, some dim lustre of the great legend"(I,244). In formal dress she strikes his imagination as "some silver coin of the Renaissance" or "a goddess" or "sea-nymph waist-high in the summer surge. Above all she suggested to him the reflexion that the *femme du monde*—in these finest developments of the type—was, like Cleopatra in the play, indeed various and multifold"(I,270–271)'.

Hints abound that Strether appreciates without coolly analyzing Madame de Vionnet, and the figures of the "goddess still partly engaged in a morning cloud" and the partly hidden "sea-nymph" delicately suggest the chaste boundaries of Strether's fertile imagination.[5] When he sees her praying in

5. U. C. Knoepflmacher makes this subtle point about the errors of Strether's "purifying" imagination (" 'O Rare for Strether!': *Antony and Cleopatra* and *The Ambassadors*," *Nineteenth-Century Fiction,* 19 [March 1965], 333–344). But analysis in general, as I have argued in my chapter on *The Sacred Fount,* is a complexly viewed activity in James's work. Here one feels, along with Maria Gostrey, that it would probably impede appreciation more than it would enhance knowledge.

Notre Dame, "she reminded our friend—since it was the way of nine tenths of his current impressions to act as recalls of things imagined—of some fine firm concentrated heroine of an old story"(II,6). His imagination associates her with the heroines of Victor Hugo, finds her "romantic . . . far beyond what she could have guessed"(II,9); and he intuitively decides that "unassailably innocent was a relation that could make one of the parties to it so carry herself"(II,10).

Such analogies from the world of art suffuse *The Ambassadors*. This one both echoes the London melodrama Strether witnessed with Maria (which corroborated his melodramatic vision of Chad's affair) and prefigures his identification of rural France with the never-attained Lambeint of his youth. Considering the novel in this light, Richard Poirier generalizes: "*The Ambassadors* offers remarkably beautiful instances of the hero's effort to transform the things he sees into visions, to detach them from time and from the demands of nature, and to give them the composition of *objets d'art*. The novel is about the cost and profit for such acts of imagination."[6]

The most suggestive allusion is the one to Cleopatra, for it hints at both Madame de Vionnet's rich sexual vitality (which he ignores) and her inscrutable "mixture of lucidity and mystery. She fell in at moments with the theory about her he most cherished, and she seemed at others to blow it into air. She spoke now as if her art were all an innocence, and then again as if her innocence were all an art"(II,115–116). Enchantingly beyond analysis, she exerts the same influence on Strether's imagination that Paris does, "a jewel brilliant and hard, in which parts were not to be discriminated nor differences comfortably marked. It twinkled and trembled and melted together, and what seemed all surface one moment seemed all depth the next"(I,89). This mixture of appreciation and error in his vision of Madame de Vionnet characterizes the general attempt of his imagination to fathom

6. Poirier, *World Elsewhere,* p. 124.

the appearances that confront him. We might now measure how far he travels from his Woollett stereotypes, yet how distant he remains from Parisian sophistication.

When Strether marvels at the unexpected change in Chad after the encounter in the theater, Maria is impatient at his not having "seen" the female influence:

> She got up from her chair, at this, with a nearer approach than she had ever yet shown to dismay at his dimness. She even, fairly pausing for it, spoke with a shade of pity. "Guess!"
> It was a shade, fairly, that brought a flush into his face; so that for a moment . . . their difference was between them. "You mean that just your hour with him told you so much of his story? Very good; I'm not such a fool, on my side, as that I don't understand you, or as that I didn't in some degree understand him. That he has done what he liked most isn't, among any of us, a matter the least in dispute. There's equally little question at this time of day of what it is he does like most. But I'm not talking," he reasonably explained, "of any mere wretch he may still pick up. I'm talking of some person who in his present situation may have held her own, may really have counted"[I,169].

The "difference between them" is of course his ignorance of the positive role a sexual relation has played in Chad's development, and Strether, a little piqued by her pity, goes on to articulate his thought. He knows that Chad has an unfortunate *faible* for "mere wretches," but—James with mild irony has him "reasonably" explain—such a woman wouldn't account for the change in Chad. Although Strether's categories are gently mocked and his imagination is in error, he has still made an impressive stride. If he is confused as to the vehicle for Chad's improvement, it is because he now appreciates the scope and value of the improvement.

Later he will tell little Bilham:

> "She keeps *him* up—she keeps the whole thing up . . . She's wonderful, wonderful, as Miss Barrace says; and he is, in his

way, too; however, as a mere man, he may sometimes rebel and not feel that he finds his account in it. She has simply given him an immense moral lift, and what that can explain is prodigious. That's why I speak of it as a situation. It *is* one, if ever there was." And Strether, with his head back and his eyes on the ceiling, seemed to lose himself in the vision of it.

His companion attended deeply. "You state it much better than I could"[I,284].

The mistake in Strether's "vision of it" is the same as in the earlier passage, but something remarkable has happened. Though Strether's imagination balks at the physical basis of Chad and Madame de Vionnet's relationship, in his own way he now does full—even ideal—justice to their affair. Smugness and complacency have disappeared from his tone, and in their place is appreciative wonder. Having brooded at length upon their affair, Strether succeeds in expressing it as a formed, consistent, dramatic "situation." He has imagined it with a rightness that transcends his factual error, and little Bilham says no more than the truth.

Strether's mounting perception of the motives and behavior of those around him begins to bear fruit. Waymarsh, he makes out, will have cabled Mrs. Newsome about her ambassador's truancy. Maria wonders if this angers Strether, and he calmly replies, "Do I look in a great rage?"(II,39). He goes on thoughtfully to piece together Waymarsh's rationale: "He has acted from the deepest conviction, with the best conscience and after wakeful nights"(II,39–40). Maria, who may remember Strether's earlier indignant description of the "base, venal" woman, is struck by his tone of civilized lucidity and imaginative sympathy: "How wonderfully you take it! But you're always wonderful"(II,40).

With his growing ability to penetrate appearances and to appreciate motives, Strether escapes the frightened insecurity, though not the discomfort, of his "double consciousness," and as the situation deteriorates he remains equal to its complications. When Waymarsh tells him Sarah is about to descend, he reflects: "Considering how many pieces had to fit themselves, it all fell, in Strether's brain, into a close rapid order. He saw on the spot what had happened, and what probably would yet; and it was all funny enough. It was perhaps just this freedom of appreciation that wound him up to his flare of high spirits. 'What is she coming *for?*—to kill me?' "(II,188).

This intrepid urbanity, this daring to imagine and thus confront things he would earlier have avoided, has already warned Strether that Jim's silence in the taxi portends a general failure of perception on the part of the new ambassadors. Jim, furthermore, who is to convey unwittingly to Chad the ignominious fate of the Woollett businessman, "tells" Strether more in twenty minutes than he had in as many years: "He seemed to say that there was a whole side of life on which the perfectly usual *was* for leading Woollett business-men to be out of the question . . . Strether's imagination, as always, worked, and he asked himself if this side of life were not somehow connected, for those who figured on it, with the fact of marriage. Would *his* relation to it, had he married ten years before, have become now the same as Pocock's?"(II,82). Inevitably approaching nearer and nearer to the main source of his uneasiness, Strether's expanding imagination closes with Mrs. Newsome herself; immovable and filled with her inadequate vision of things, *she* cannot be altered: " 'What it comes to [if one wants to change her]' said Strether, 'is that you've got morally and intellectually to get rid of her' "(II,239).

With his perception thus sharpened, Strether cannot help foreseeing that Chad will eventually leave it all to him: "I 'sort of' feel . . . that the whole thing will come upon me. Yes, I shall have every inch and every ounce of it. I shall be *used* for it—! . . . To the last drop of my blood"(II,140). Consequently, Chad's reiterated declarations of faith sound ominously hollow to Strether's "imaginative mind"(II,211).

He sees that the young man will soon grow tired of Madame de Vionnet, and Chad's make-believe kick of the imaginary bribe further chills Strether with the impression of a "restless" boy doing "an irrelevant hornpipe or jig"(II,218).

Virtually doomed to know all, Strether is helpless before his penetrating imagination. When Chad and Madame de Vionnet come floating down the river into his ken, he sees immediately and entirely what they are even before identifying who they are:

For two very happy persons he found himself straightway taking them—a young man in shirt-sleeves, a young woman easy and fair, who had pulled pleasantly up from some other place and, being acquainted with the neighbourhood, had known what this particular retreat could offer them. The air quite thickened, at their approach, with further intimations; the intimation that they were expert, familiar, frequent—that this wouldn't at all events be the first time. They knew how to do it, he vaguely felt . . . [II,256].

The insistent impression of their familiarity with the neighborhood, with the inn, with themselves; the loosely sexual reference of "expert, familiar, frequent"; the heavily sexual implications of "this wouldn't at all events be the first time. They knew how to do it"—all these pitiless notations of Strether's unerring, educated imagination will remain lodged in his memory to point up, by contrast, the peculiar ignorance that also characterizes his imagination. The man who expertly takes in every detail of their intimacy, their annoyance, and their considering whether to "cut" him if he has not seen them is the same man who "almost blushed, in the dark, for the way he had dressed the possibility in vagueness, as a little girl might have dressed her doll . . . He recognized at last that he had really been trying all along to suppose nothing"(II,266).

To analyze Strether's experience apart from his imagination is to invite artificial distinctions. Strether's behavior and his vision are so intimately related—and both are so fully developed in this novel ("behavior" was conspicuously limited in *The Sacred Fount*)—that any final view of the novel is obliged to discuss them together. At this point, however, it seems worthwhile to attempt to isolate the curve of Strether's Parisian experience, its arc of deepening initiation and modified withdrawal.

Before joining Maria Gostrey in the garden at Chester, Strether reflects on the oddness of his position and on the sense of being launched in something new: "It had begun in fact already upstairs and before the dressing-glass . . . begun with a sharper survey of the elements of Appearance than he had for a long time been moved to make"(I,9). His own physical appearance and that of others, the phenomena about him, begin to take on a mixed and intensifying interest. When he first enters Maria's Parisian apartment, his response is a characteristic compound of admiration expressed in Biblical phrases that simultaneously imply mistrust: "wide as his glimpse had lately become of the empire of 'things,' what was before him still enlarged it; the lust of the eyes and the pride of life had indeed thus their temple"(I,119). He becomes so initiated, however, into this source of pleasure that, when he later visits Madame de Vionnet's apartment, his appreciative faculties cause him to sense about her possessions "the air of supreme respectability, the consciousness . . . of private honour" (I,245–246).

Nevertheless, Strether remains intermittently uncomfortable until he has an idea of what lies beneath the surfaces, what they conceal. Parisian conversation is vividly entertaining, but he wonders if it has, as in the metamorphosis of Waymarsh into Sitting Bull, any relation to truth: "You've all of you here so much visual sense that you've somehow all 'run' to it. There are moments when it strikes one that you haven't any other"(I,206). When Miss Barrace whimsically agrees with his charge: "in the light of Paris one sees what things resemble . . . Everything, every one shows," Strether cannot resist asking, "But for what they really are?" to which she responds, "Oh I like your Boston 'really's'!"(I,207). Charming people, delightful manners, playful conversations—she implies—convey their own meanings; and Strether must learn—like Maisie and the narrator of *The Sacred Fount*—to interpret such phenomena by their appearances alone rather than seek helplessly to discover the essences "really" within. And every now and then, as with the inscrutable Paris where "what seemed all surface one moment seemed all depth the next"(I,89), he receives a slight jolt: "He made out in a moment that the youth was in earnest as he hadn't yet seen him; which in its turn threw a ray perhaps a trifle startling on what they had each up to that time been treating as earnestness"(I,234).

Strether's growing appreciation of the physical world is also conveyed, as other critics have noted, by the mounting pleasure he takes in meals during his experience of Europe. Dining with Maria Gostrey by candlelight in London, Strether takes in "the rose-coloured shades and the small table and the soft fragrance of the lady—had anything to his mere sense ever been so soft?"(I,50). Rising to the occasion, his "mere sense" proceeds to give way to the "uncontrolled perception that his friend's velvet band somehow added, in her appearance, to the value of every other item—to that of her smile and of the way she carried her head, to that of her complexion, of her lips, her teeth, her eyes, her hair"(I,50–51). It is an observation and a catalogue Strether would have blushed to make earlier; desire and the appreciation of the human figure as something potentially lovely are awakening. "The lust of the eyes and the pride of life," moreover, are everywhere on display when he arrives in Paris. The aroma of sensuous nature groomed by art is wafted to Strether by the Parisian breeze: "the air had a taste as of something mixed with art, something that presented nature as a white-capped master-chef"(I,79).

The epitome of the artful though simple perfection of the

sensuous Parisian life is expressed—again in terms of a meal—through Strether's unforgettable luncheon with Madame de Vionnet at the restaurant on the quay:

He was to feel many things on this occasion, and one of the first of them was that he had travelled far since that evening in London, before the theatre, when his dinner with Maria Gostrey . . . had struck him as requiring so many explanations. He had at that time gathered them in, the explanations . . . but it was at present as if he had either soared above or sunk below them . . . he could somehow think of none that didn't seem to leave the appearance of collapse and cynicism easier for him than lucidity. How could he wish it to be lucid for others, for any one, that he, for the hour, saw reasons enough in the mere way the bright clean ordered waterside life came in at the open window?—the mere way Madame de Vionnet, opposite him over their intensely white table-linen, their *omelette aux tomates,* their bottle of straw-coloured Chablis, thanked him for everything almost with the smile of a child, while her grey eyes moved in and out of their talk, back to the quarter of the warm spring air, in which early summer had already begun to throb, and then back again to his face and their human questions[II,13–14].

The woman, the city, the food blend together and move him in a way that, he now feels, no explanation can account for. As overpoweringly real, attractive, self-justifying phenomena, they mean more than any abstraction in the form of a moral tag that can be leveled for or against them. It is only "the appearance of collapse and cynicism," a necessary step in the process of conversion that Strether—like little Bilham before him—undergoes, as his inadequate moral props fall beneath him and he begins to appreciate the sheer sensuous joy of sharing a simple—though elegant—meal, in a charming setting with an ardent woman.[7] In so doing he shows how

7. In a generalization with which I am almost entirely in accord, Richard Poirier interprets the "conversion" motif: "*The Ambassadors* is essentially about the process enacted in Gloriani's garden, the process of 'conversion': the failed 'conversion' of Chad by Madame de Vionnet, the 'conversion' of Strether by Paris into a man whose capacities for appreciation create a world—alternative both to Paris and to Woollett

far he has come toward the "single boon" he desires, "the common unattainable art of taking things as they came"(I,83).

Through being able to take Madame de Vionnet as she is, though this smashes his categories, he gains immeasurably in appreciation. When Sarah Pocock later lashes out at him, "Do you consider her even an apology for a decent woman?" he thinks to himself, "Ah there it was at last! . . . It was so much—so much; and she treated it, poor lady, as so little"(II,201–202). The phrase "poor lady" turns out not to be wholly figurative; it is rigid and unappreciative Sarah Pocock, like Mrs. Touchett in *The Portrait of a Lady,* who is finally impoverished. The Cleopatra allusion for Madame de Vionnet is variously suggestive, as several critics have pointed out, but in no way more so than in indicating the impoverishment of not knowing Madame de Vionnet:

Antony: Would I had never seen her!
Enobarbus: O, sir, you had then left unseen a wonderful piece of
　　　　　work; which not to have been blest withal would
　　　　　have discredited your travel.
　　　　　　　　　　[*Antony and Cleopatra,* I,ii,158–161].

Such a change in Strether has its source in his encountering and being altered by phenomena more inscrutable and lovely than any he has seen before. He returns from an early conversation with little Bilham and reports gaily to Waymarsh, "Well, I guess I don't know anything!" Learning that little Bilham has passed this bit of information on to Strether, Waymarsh is annoyed, but Strether considers it not as a reduction but as "somehow enlarging," something he has "found out from

---

and more compelling in the duties it demands from him than either place could be." (*World Elsewhere,* pp. 130–131.) While Poirier focuses upon the alternative world itself, I am more interested in the implications of its distance from both Paris and Woollett.

the young man"(I,106). All of the toddling and rebirth metaphors associated with Strether point to his voluntary acceptance of a blank slate; Waymarsh, of course, never toddles. Thus prepared, Strether recognizes and richly appreciates Chad's transformation: "One wants, confound it, don't you see? . . . to enjoy anything so rare." "With such elements," he knows, "one can't count"(I,167–168), can't analyze; just as, "thanks to one of the short-cuts of genius, she [Madame de Vionnet] had taken all his categories by surprise"(I,271).

Shorn of his categories, Strether relies only on his individual faculty of appreciation, a faculty that depends upon context and cannot operate by remote control or across the sea. Mrs. Newsome cannot possibly appreciate Madame de Vionnet, because, as Strether has learned, "there's all the indescribable—what one gets only on the spot"(II,126). When pressed by Sarah to account for himself, Strether's response is correspondingly uncategorical, not "lucid," but deeply appropriate:

I don't think there's anything I've done in any such calculated way as you describe. Everything has come as a sort of indistinguishable part of everything else. Your coming out belonged closely to my having come before you, and my having come was a result of our general state of mind. Our general state of mind had proceeded, on its side, from our queer ignorance, our queer misconceptions and confusions—from which, since then, an inexorable tide of light seems to have floated us into our perhaps still queerer knowledge[II,200–201].

What he has done is, devastatingly, to see for himself. "I couldn't, without my own impression, realise. She's a tremendously clever brilliant capable woman, and with an extraordinary charm on top of it all . . . I understand what a relation with such a woman—what such a high fine friendship—may be. It can't be vulgar or coarse, anyway—and that's the point"(I,280).

Strether, of course, pays for such an impression, but not primarily because it is partly false nor because he will lose the security that otherwise awaits his return home. He pays most dearly, from beginning to end, because it is an impression, as he is well aware, that betrays a woman to whom he owes much and who has every reason, given her views and his commitment, to expect different behavior from him.

Nevertheless, confronting and accepting such a cost, Strether faces up to his new and "fatal perceptions" and begins to "let go." Since "he might perish by the sword as well as by famine"(I,115), he decides to enjoy some of those things, including smoking with a lady, that he somehow never had occasion to do earlier. Little Bilham and Waymarsh both receive his impassioned counsel to live, and, having "missed the train" all his life, he catches, on the spur of the moment, a random one to the country. Wandering through the pastoral woods, he lounges luxuriantly about and freely chatters to himself in French, unhampered by the critical eye of others. Responding to artful appearances and the joys of sensuous living, forgetting his troublesome moral categories, nurturing his faculty of appreciation and finding that his desires themselves have been growing, Strether completes this stage of his initiation into European experience with a leisurely and elaborate celebration of his awakened appetite for life. He orders a sumptuous "repast" at the pastoral Cheval Blanc and, mentally savoring the feast to come, retires to the garden with his aperitif to enjoy the view of the river.

Before considering Strether's encounter with Chad and Madame de Vionnet, one further pattern of initiation must be traced: the transformation from spectator to performer. An elderly man half enviously, half complacently observing a world of strange, brilliant appearances is Strether's first conception of himself. He feels obliged to warn Maria Gostrey, "I come from Woollett Massachusetts." When she probes into the reasons for this warning, he answers, "Why that you should find me too hopeless"(I,14–15).

At the London theater with her as his guide, Strether is already becoming rejuvenated, but he is still awed by the performance at which he is a mere spectator. Characteristically he misjudges the melodrama he sees, regarding it as a work of art, just as later he will be aware of the artistic beauty of Chad's affair, initially regarded as a melodrama. The theater itself, Strether reflects, is a dubious source of entertainment for Mrs. Newsome's supposedly austere and authoritative ambassador: "He clearly hadn't come out in the name of propriety but to visit unattended equivocal performances"(I,88–89). During another such "equivocal performance," Chad makes his fabulous stage entry, and Strether is clearly all agog, the fascinated spectator. At Gloriani's garden party and in Notre Dame, likewise, Strether plays the role of observer in the pageant of life unfolding itself.

A significant shift in sympathy, however, has taken place. Regretting the emptiness of his own youth, Strether now assents to what he sees and decides that, though he is too old for "the affair of life," he will do what he can for Madame de Vionnet, will "give her a sign. The sign would be that—though it was her own affair—he understood; the sign would be that—though it was her own affair—she was free to clutch. Since she took him for a firm object . . . he would do his best to *be* one"(II,11). Caught between his intense desire to help and his multiple awareness that he is too old, that he is elsewhere committed, and that he knows both more and less than he ought to about "her own affair," Strether makes a cautious, in some ways unwilling and uninformed, but profound commitment to the new appearances. He steps into the act, and before long his nightmares are not of failing Mrs. Newsome but of failing Madame de Vionnet through a craven surrender to Sarah Pocock(II,61).

At the luncheon with Madame de Vionnet he takes from her an explanation of this new commitment more acute and concise than any he could proffer:

"But for myself," she added, "the question is what *you* make."
"Ah I make nothing. It's not my affair."
"I beg your pardon. It's just there that, since you've taken it up and are committed to it, it most intensely becomes yours. You're not saving me, I take it, for your interest in myself, but for your interest in our friend. The one's at any rate wholly dependent on the other. You can't in honour not see me through," she wound up, "because you can't in honour not see *him*"[II,22].

Although she ignores or tactfully minimizes his interest in her as a motive, Madame de Vionnet unerringly points to the vision of Chad that Strether has, to the hilt, appreciated. Strether is "committed" indeed—he's up to his neck in the "affair"— because of the way, as her last words richly suggest, he has *seen* Chad. Imaginative vision thus fuses with Strether's active experience; seeing Chad leads "in honour" to seeing him through.

At Sarah's hotel room he recognizes instantly how compromised he is. Already convicted of being in Madame de Vionnet's boat, he has no options: "He took up an oar and, since he was to have the credit of pulling, pulled"(II,94–95). Unmistakably active now, Strether shows how well he has assimilated the sophisticated and playful art of European manners. Madame de Vionnet, never more a *femme du monde* than now, engages in delightful, exaggerated love-play with Strether: "When does one ever see you? I wait at home and I languish. You'll have rendered me the service, Mrs. Pocock, at least . . . of giving me one of my much-too-rare glimpses of this gentleman"(II,99).

Doubtless hearing for the first time the word "languish" used in connection with "Mr. Strether," Sarah, slightly unnerved, grants Madame de Vionnet her "natural due" and

147

asserts that "the privilege of his society isn't a thing I shall quarrel about with any one." Gaily and intrepidly ignoring the unpleasant connotations of her remark, Strether leaps into the breach: "And yet, dear Sarah . . . I feel, when I hear you say that, that you don't quite do justice to the important truth of the extent to which—as you're also mine—I'm *your* natural due. I should like much better . . . to see you fight for me"(II,99–100)'. A seasoned actor now, he accepts Madame de Vionnet's caressing attention and innuendo, reflecting that "it was indeed as if they were arranged, gathered for a performance, the performance of 'Europe' by his confederate and himself. Well the performance could only go on"(II,105)'.

The performance does go on, and, instead of passively or blankly watching it, Strether is one of the stage managers, one of the few truly "in it" who perceive the hidden motive behind Chad's dazzling round of parties for his family. Miss Barrace, who habitually confuses Strether, joins with him now to "embroider the theme" of the delightful drama they're watching: "Oh I see the principle. If one didn't one would be lost. But when once one has got hold of it—"(II,176)'. Their language, one notices, echoes the tutored Mrs. Briss of *The Sacred Fount* when she begins to "perceive," among the bewildering appearances before them, the hidden motives offered by the narrator: "When one knows it, it's all there. But what's that vulgar song?—'You've got to know it first!'" "When one has had the 'tip' one looks back and sees things in a new light" (*The Sacred Fount*, 56, 59)'. No similarity points up contrasts more effectively than this one; the obsessive epistemological theme of *The Sacred Fount* is strictly subordinated to the larger concerns of the story in *The Ambassadors:* one has no doubt whatsoever that Strether and Miss Barrace *do* know. Earlier he would have been baffled, but Strether now not only understands the spectacle of European manners, he is credited, again by Miss Barrace, with being the indispensable performer of them all, the one on whom it all depends: "We know you as the hero of the drama, and we're gathered to see what you'll do"(II,179).

Of course what complicates our response to Strether is our knowledge that if he is "the hero," he does not entirely understand the nature of "the drama" in which he participates. Appearances, after all, "must have a basis"(II,300), and this basis Strether has consistently, almost willfully misunderstood. Europe is delightful, but at moments he sees through its charming facade: "Then there was something in the great world covertly tigerish, which came to him across the lawn and in the charming air as a waft from the jungle"(I,219). Behind the dazzling manners of Gloriani's sophisticated garden party, he senses the interplay of veiled passions. Again, when Madame de Vionnet informs him of her calculated plan to "bring off" Jeanne's marriage, Strether inwardly winces: "Vaguely and confusedly he was troubled by it . . . He had allowed for depths, but these were greater . . . It was—through something ancient and cold in it—what he would have called the real thing"(II,129).

One thinks of Osmond and Madame Merle attempting to "bring off" Pansy's marriage to Lord Warburton. But where that situation really was "hideous and unclean," Strether's uneasiness at the European convention of planned marriages seems to reflect as much on the incompleteness of his "Europeanized" state as on the brutality of the convention itself.

Strether determinedly throws off these moments of discomfiture. He prefers to view European appearances and traditions romantically, as emblems of western civilization to be enjoyed and artistically embroidered by the appreciative imagination. Nowhere is such embroidering more in evidence than during his day of pastoral rambling. Here the various motifs of romance culminate.

Throughout the novel Strether has vicariously re-created his youth, and his trip to the country—in which he catches the train he had always missed—seems to actualize what had at first been metaphorical. Strether lives into the Lambinet painting he could not afford to buy years earlier: "it was all there, in short—it was what he wanted: it was Tremont Street, it was France, it was Lambinet. Moreover he was freely walking about in it"(II,247). Not only does his youth seem to be recaptured and redeemed, but art and life come together; the rural scene "fell into a composition, full of felicity"(II,247) such as only art or life perfected by form can offer. It all thus harmonizes with his vision of Chad as like a "pleasant perfect work of art"(II,79), with his vision of Madame de Vionnet as a mythological goddess, and with his sense of the Parisian air as the perfecting instrument for lifting sensuous life into formal art.

He comfortably muses about the new role Madame de Vionnet now plays in his life, the pleasant danger of falling in love with her, the increasing intimacy between the two of them, with Chad "out of the picture." Strether himself remains all day in the picture, not once overstepping "the oblong gilt frame"(II,252); and he reflects on what was at bottom its spell: "that it was essentially more than anything else a scene and a stage, that the very air of the play was in the rustle of the willows and the tone of the sky"(II,253). Having participated in "the performance of Europe," Strether feels familiar with the drama before him, and he enjoys deeply both the difference between this "picture" and Woollett and his own confidence in being able "to make one's account with what one lighted on"(II,254).

Settling down for dinner at the Cheval Blanc, Strether reflects "that the picture and the play seemed supremely to melt together in the good woman's broad sketch of what she could do for her visitor's appetite"(II,254). Appetite, picture, and play; youth and age; a sense of being initiated into European life and into the teasing possibility of love; the fusion of pastoral art and rural French life—all these come together before the moment of Strether's climactic meal, only to separate, a few minutes later, at the appearance of the real lovers. The romance has been true, he sees, in his mind alone: he is not a young lover, though he may muse about the possibility; he is not in Madame de Vionnet's boat, though he may pull the oars as much as he wishes. The pastoral artistry emanates as much from himself as from the scene; the real drama—not the imagined picture—is one, finally, for which "he knew he had been, at bottom, neither prepared nor proof"(II,261–262).

The meal the three eat together is but a shadow of that sumptuous feast he had confidently ordered a few minutes earlier; his "appetite," so to speak, has received a deathblow. "There had been simply a *lie* in the charming affair—a lie on which one could now, detached and deliberate, perfectly put one's finger. It was with the lie that they had eaten and drunk and talked and laughed . . ."(II,262–263). He sees now, as Madame de Vionnet weaves a story out of thin air, the artifice involved in their art and in his artistic, embroidering imagination: "What it all came to had been that fiction and fable *were,* inevitably, in the air, and not as a simple term of comparison, but as a result of things said"(II,262).

Yet the decorous lie is still preferable to any vulgar rending of veils: "He had had in the actual case to make-believe more than he liked, but this was nothing, it struck him, to what the other event would have required. Could he, literally, quite have faced the other event?"(II,265). Increasingly thankful for the grace of her behavior under stress, Strether comes to realize "that their eminent 'lie,' Chad's and hers, was simply after all such an inevitable tribute to good taste as he couldn't have wished them not to render . . . he could trust her to make deception right. As she presented things the ugliness—goodness knew why—went out of them"(II,277). Strether's present attitude toward the Parisian world of intriguing appearances is a precarious balance of trust and disenchantment. The difficulty of maintaining such a balance is increased, moreover, by his gradual discovery of the liabilities of his imagination and of the cost of the kind of living he had earlier exhorted little Bilham to attain.

The exemplar of ideal "living" has, of course, been Chad, and Strether's developing attitude toward him greatly influences the shape of Strether's own behavior. The elder man's first impression was of a transcendent, miraculous change. Chad has become a smooth and polished man of the world, one "to whom things had happened and were variously known"(I,152). He has been artistically formed, "put into a firm mould and turned successfully out"(I,152). Strether immediately correlates this with his vision of Chad as "the young man marked out by women; and for a concentrated minute the dignity, the comparative austerity . . . of this character affected him almost with awe . . . Yes, experience was what Chad did play on him"(II,153,155).

Chad has lived, Strether intuits, in those undefined and exciting ways *he* never knew, and they remain undefined for several reasons. Strether can only guess at Chad's achievement, since it corresponds to a vague yearning rather than a precise knowledge. Encounters with women; a casual self-possession; expressive, graceful, assured manners; doing easily what one likes; being the center of relations in which the other parties are pleased to play "subsidiary" roles; enjoying and being "expert, familiar" with the spectacle of life; above all knowing "how to do it"—these are hazily inferred by Strether as components of Chad's awesome experience. But there are reasons beyond Strether's inevitable vagueness for the novel's refusal to substantiate in greater detail Chad's achievement; this achievement is seriously called into question as the novel progresses; James never intended the reader to respond to it as entirely solid.

Beyond this, I would suggest, lies James's refusal ever to create a convincing image of experience composed in the terms of Chad's presumed achievement. Strether may yearn for those achievements, may passionately urge little Bilham not to miss them, but James never, as a novelist, makes them credible. They are rendered hazily because they are not a viable value in the Jamesian world. The Chad Newsomes in his fiction are not shown attaining their experience, and the internal logic within James's novels succeeds ultimately in casting doubt on the very goals of such characters. It is as though twenty-five years earlier James faced the novelistic (and perhaps personal) choice of pursuing the kind of experience available to Roderick or the kind available to Rowland. As I suggested earlier, the Roderick figure does reappear in James's fiction, but it is to those toward whom he is tender—Newman at the very end, Isabel, Ralph Touchett, Hyacinth, Maisie, Milly, but not Chad—that James grants the superior imagination and disillusionment, the distinctive, perhaps compulsive experience of a life filled with perception and deprived of all else that he first embodied in Rowland Mallet. Strether, one finally sees, can no more attain, or ultimately endorse, Chad's experience than Rowland can Roderick's.

To live as Chad lives, in the rich possession of passion and intimacy, is, throughout James's fiction, to create costs and impose burdens that, once imaginatively realized, James's distinctive heroes can never permit themselves. If one is to live like Chad, one cannot imagine and respond like Strether; if one is to appreciate with Strether's full intensity, one must forego the shared intimacy and experience of Chad's way of life. It is the salient feature of James's moral world that physical experience and activity are presented (and in some cases distorted) in such a way as to be inaccessible to his imaginative heroes and heroines. Strether will learn about Chad what Isabel Archer finally perceives about herself: "to take a deep, self-developing breath is, morally speaking, to cause those nearby almost to suffocate" (see above, Chapter Two).

Chad's "acquired high polish" involves a considerable amount of "hardness" (II,65), and Strether increasingly realizes the difficulty of moving the young man into alignment with

Strether's vision of him. Chad is his own man, handles things his own way, listens to Strether without responding to him. Such inscrutable, self-absorbed, inflexible self-possession leads Strether anew to realize "the truth that everything came happily back with him to his knowing how to live . . . He [Strether] didn't want, luckily, to prevent Chad from living, but he was quite aware that even if he had he would himself have thoroughly gone to pieces. It was in truth essentially by bringing down his personal life to a function all subsidiary to the young man's own that he held together"(II,212).

The tone of the passage is slightly ambiguous toward Chad's unique gift. "Living," as the younger man exemplifies it, increasingly resembles exploiting, and Strether's perception of Chad's behavior at the Cheval Blanc completes the revolution of his own point of view: "It was a part of the deep impression for Strether . . . that Chad in particular could let her know he left it to her. He habitually left things to others, as Strether was so well aware, and it in fact came over our friend in these meditations that there had been as yet no such vivid illustration of his famous knowing how to live"(II,263–264).

As his vision of Chad darkens, so, in a more complicated way, does his idealized version of Madame de Vionnet. When, flushed, she breaks into French at the Cheval Blanc, he sees her as, after all, a Frenchwoman speaking her language as millions of others do. At the same time he appreciates her rare talent for making "deception right," the "tribute to good taste" that her charming fictions express. But it is at Madame de Vionnet's apartment, for the last time, that his vision of her clarifies itself. Desperate over her coming loss she clings to and even—a little—pretends a romantic interest in Strether to keep him by her in Paris.

It is a difficult scene to interpret, and Madame de Vionnet may not be pretending at all. Her words to Strether are impassioned and sound sincere, but it is hard not to accept Strether's view that Chad is at the center of her feelings and he, Strether, is appealed to as a temporary refuge and pawn. Still, Strether's reinforced detachment and his sexual timidity probably blind him to the degree of candor actually behind her outburst; he has lavished upon her an appreciative admiration that no one else, not even Chad, has shown, and it causes her genuine anguish to lose, as she thinks, his respect. The mixture in her of sex and affection, of art and innocence has always baffled Strether, and probably never more than now. He is more perturbed by this apparent duplicity than by what he had discovered in the country, and he intuitively senses the source of her trouble:

What was at bottom the matter with her, embroider as she might and disclaim as she might . . . was simply Chad himself. It was of Chad she was after all renewedly afraid; the strange strength of her passion was the very strength of her fear; she clung to *him,* Lambert Strether, as to a source of safety she had tested, and, generous graceful truthful as she might try to be, exquisite as she was, she dreaded the term of his being within reach. With this sharpest perception yet, it was like a chill in the air to him, it was almost appalling, that a creature so fine could be, by mysterious forces, a creature so exploited[II,284].

What brings her down, what keeps her from being quite as "generous graceful truthful" as he had once imagined is just that "strange strength of her passion" which he now discerns beneath her charm, analogous to that earlier glimpse of passion lurking beneath the splendid pageant of manners in Gloriani's garden. It chills and almost appalls him that even she is compromised "by mysterious forces" beyond her control, "exploited" by the current of her feelings for Chad, a victim— and to that degree vulgar—of her own desires. Exploited by her own passion, she will, he thinks, in the most well-intended but also desperate way, exploit him as a means of solacing herself or keeping Chad by her. He sees for the first time and tells her that she's afraid for her life.

At this she breaks down, and as he witnesses her torment he almost ceases to think of her personally at all—

as if he could think of nothing but the passion, mature, abysmal, pitiful, she represented, and the possibilities she betrayed. She was older for him tonight, visibly less exempt from the touch of time; but she was as much as ever the finest and subtlest creature, the happiest apparition, it had been given him, in all his years, to meet; and yet he could see her there as vulgarly troubled, in very truth, as a maidservant crying for her young man. The only thing was she judged herself as the maidservant wouldn't; the weakness of which wisdom, the dishonour of which judgment, seemed but to sink her lower[II,286].

Like the narrator of *The Sacred Fount* reflecting on May Server, Strether—sympathetic but quite detached and resolutely passive now—sees Madame de Vionnet less as a person than a "wasted and dishonoured symbol" of "the possibilities of our common nature" (*Fount,* 107). When he does see her as a person, it is to note her bondage to time and passion, to her physical condition as a human being. While the ethereal emblem of French civilization is timeless, the flesh and blood woman he sees before him is "vulgarly" distraught, like "a maidservant crying for her young man." Worse, she is unfortunate enough to judge herself by a "higher" standard, without being able to alter the course on which her passions have led her, and this "seemed but to sink her lower." What he most recoils from, however, what he considers "the real coercion" is "to see a man ineffably adored"(II,285). Just as "a man" has no business, in the light of Strether's sensibilities, being "ineffably adored," so, in equally generic terms, does the revelation of intimacy disturb him: "intimacy, at such a point, was *like* that—and what in the world else would one have wished it to be like?"(II,266).

The whole business of physical human intimacy goes obscurely against his loftier conceptions of human behavior; what he had indeed expected, as she so painfully sensed, was that she would be "well, sublime!"(II,288). With its connotation of ethereality, "sublime" is the appropriate word for Strether's vision of human beings who have, he imagines, risen beyond their physical desires. It is part of that ideal pastoral fusion of nature and art that came to an end at the Cheval Blanc, a fusion that Strether, like Isabel, must believe in before he can so ardently expound the gospel of "living." With the downfall of his palace of thought, he retreats, slightly but significantly, into the role in which he will remain—the sympathetic but detached observer. Experience has been wonderful but never quite so grand as that vision of it created by his imagination, and, when Madame de Vionnet declares, "I've wanted you too," he answers truthfully, "Ah but you've *had* me!"(II,289). For imaginative intimacy is the only plane on which he can consent to be "had"; from any other form of intimacy—with Madame de Vionnet and later with Maria Gostrey—he gently but firmly withdraws.

Playfully accepting Strether's "daring" invitation to luncheon on the quay, Madame de Vionnet had remarked that "her affairs would go to smash, but hadn't one a right to one's snatch of scandal when one was prepared to pay?"(II,13). A great deal of Strether's experience is concerned with perceiving the ugliness of unpaid debts and the expense of paid ones. The most damning aspect of Mrs. Newsome's and the Pococks' blindness is that they want the finished product safe at home again, without paying the artist for her labors. "The business [of effecting Chad's transformation] hadn't been easy; it had taken time and trouble, it had cost, above all, a price" (II,65–66). The price—Chad's relationship with Madame de Vionnet—is what they refuse to consider; moreover, Chad gives signs of ignoring it himself. Strether reminds him that "more has been done for you, I think, than I've ever seen done . . . by one human being for another"(II,224). Sure of failure at the end, he helplessly upbraids Chad, "You'll be a brute, you know—you'll be guilty of the last infamy—if you ever forsake her"(II,308).

But Strether himself is in a similar predicament; quite like Chad, he is reminded by Maria Gostrey: "Well, you owe more to women than any man I ever saw"(II,135). The main debt he permits himself to recognize, however, is the one to Mrs. Newsome, and the honoring of it effectively shapes his last words to Maria Gostrey: "That, you see, is my only logic. Not, out of the whole affair, to have got anything for myself"(II,326). He came to Europe, his conscience insists, not for himself but as Mrs. Newsome's ambassador; he can never accept what Europe has given him for himself unless he comes home, in a sense, still as her ambassador. The "miracle" that he too has undergone would become "monstrous," like Chad's, if it were entirely at her expense. If this prevents his "living," it is because, as he becomes more and more convinced, living implies putting the burden on others' shoulders, not paying one's deepest debts.

Chad is not so transformed after all, Strether comes finally to see: "She had made him better, she had made him best, she had made him anything one would; but it came to our friend with supreme queerness that he was none the less only Chad . . . The work, however admirable, was . . . of the strict human order"(II,284). It then strikes him as "marvellous" that such a one "should be so transcendently prized" (II,284–285).

Strether, too, is finally less transformed than the reader has romantically imagined. His youth has, in a certain sense, been taken from him again; he has all along been slightly more of a confused spectator and less of an initiated actor than he had imagined; and he has found himself in a Woollett-like way shocked, "neither prepared nor proof" for his discovery at the Cheval Blanc. The exciting feeling of shared knowledge with Maria Gostrey and the Parisian sophisticates has hidden the fact that, in his innocent delusion, he has always been alone. He wonders now how he can face Maria Gostrey's "What on earth . . . had you then supposed?"(II,266). But he does face it; he resists "a revulsion in favour of the principles of Woollett"(II,296), and in a narrower sense he has indeed been transformed. The idols of his heyday, however—youth, appetite, the illusion of freedom, in a word, living—have been seriously challenged.

Youth now awakens in Strether feelings of apprehension as much as of yearning. That Chad is younger than Madame de Vionnet becomes an ominous fact, and even more ominous are Chad's youthful protestations: " 'I give you my word of honour,' he frankly rang out, 'that I'm not a bit tired of her.' Strether at this only gave him a stare; the way youth could express itself was again and again a wonder . . . he spoke of being 'tired' of her almost as he might have spoken of being tired of roast mutton for dinner"(II,312–313). Later, with some awe, Strether tells Maria, "He asks how one can dream of his being tired. But he has all life before him"(II,325). Here Chad's marvelous youth has been transformed into a vast arena for future infidelities and "affairs"; Strether stares at what "living" may yet mean for the young man.

Appetite is an ambiguous motif in the novel, since Strether's enjoyment of it has been gentle and restricted. At the Cheval Blanc his cultivation of it reaches its peak and subsides thereafter into an acceptance or understanding of others' desires. Certainly insofar as it has reference to sexual intimacy, Strether's appetite has always appeared to be moderate, and his diffidence in these matters gives point to the grotesque comedy of Jim's description of Mrs. Newsome and Sarah as voracious beasts, and of Mrs. Newsome sitting up "All night, my boy—for *you!*"(II,89). The figure of being devoured is related to the hint of something "covertly tigerish" in Gloriani's world and to the marks of passion that deface Madame de Vionnet's beauty.[8] Human passion threatens his need to be inviolate, implies an intimacy he is unwilling and unable to accept, be it from either Madame de Vionnet or Maria Gostrey.

If the illusion of freedom has any positive meaning for Strether at the end, it is surely no longer based on the vision of Chad's transformation, as his exhortation to little Bilham had been. Unrestricted self-development flourishes only at the expense of Madame de Vionnet's continuous sacrifice. The sacred fount metaphor of abysmal exploitation-sacrifice is relevant here, for it indicates how James, in his depiction of even the loveliest human intimacy, expresses primarily a dubious development and a real diminishment. Chad feels restless, wants to "live" a little more. He will neglect his unpayable debt; as little Bilham saw at the beginning, he cannot be free and good at the same time.

What it comes to is that Strether has had a vision of sublime relationships, a vision that the actual conditions can never meet. Maria tells Strether that "it would be difficult to see now quite what degree of ceremony [on the part of Chad and Madame de Vionnet] properly meets your case"(II,235). Strether concedes, "Of course, my attitude toward them is extraordinary," to which she returns, "Just so; so that one may ask one's self what style of proceeding on their part can altogether match it. The attitude of their own that won't pale in its light they've doubtless still to work out"(II,235–236). The "sublime" generosity of his imagination is, inevitably, what keeps him immaculate, isolated, doomed to disillusionment. He vanishes, in Quentin Anderson's acute phrase, into "the limbo of a lonely righteousness."[9] No "style of proceeding" can match his vision of behavior; Madame de Vionnet weeps because, merely flesh

8. For the *locus classicus* of the ravage caused by passion in James's work, one turns to the narrator's description of May Server in *The Sacred Fount:* "I saw as I had never seen before what consuming passion can make of the marked mortal on whom, with fixed beak and claws, it has settled as on a prey"(101).

9. Quentin Anderson, *The American Henry James* (New Brunswick, N.J.: Rutgers University Press, 1957), p. 221.

and blood, she cannot be "sublime." Intimacy and passion, as James sees them with their full complement of exploitation, self-surrender, anguish, and even mutilation, are to be approached through the prism of the idealizing and enriching imagination, rather than through personal experience.

Strether's unpaid debt to Maria Gostrey is the result partly of having "seen for himself" that "intimacy . . . was *like* that"(II,266) and partly of "clinging again intensely to the strength of his position, which was precisely that there was nothing in it for himself"(II,60). It is, however, a position ultimately untenable, for if Strether is right in seeing that the betrayal of Mrs. Newsome's embassy is warranted only through disinterest, he remains unjustified in entering Maria Gostrey's life, profiting greatly from her, and then discarding her when he has had his fill: "the time seemed already far off when he had held out his small thirsty cup to the spout of her pail. Her pail was scarce touched now, and other fountains had flowed for him; she fell into her place as but one of his tributaries"(II,48). This is the same prose James used to describe the sacred fount relationship—"we had suddenly caught Long in the act of presenting his receptacle at the sacred fount" (*Fount*, 32)—and it indicates the way in which Strether exploits Maria Gostrey. Ignoring his debt to her with an apparently unruffled conscience, he leaves her, in Laurence Holland's words, "in the affair of art, the affair of memory and imagination, rather than in the affair of life which she hopes for."[10]

The return to solitary spectatorship is not, after all, surprising. Strether's deepest experiences have all along been his inner vibrations to a world of marvelous appearances: "the fact was that his perception of the young man's identity . . . had been quite one of the sensations that count in life"(I,135). Even when alone, like Spencer Brydon in "The Jolly Corner," Strether can spend, while waiting for Chad, "an hour full of strange suggestions, persuasions, recognitions; one of those that he was to recall, at the end of his adventure, as the particular

10. Holland, *Expense of Vision,* p. 281.

handful that most had counted"(II,209). "It was nothing new to him . . . that a man might have—at all events such a man as he—an amount of experience out of any proportion to his adventures"(I,227).[11]

Strether lives most intensely at the level of inner response, of appreciation; and the course of the novel is to demonstrate how beautifully he rises to the spectacle of European culture: "Call it then life . . . call it poor dear old life simply that springs the surprise. Nothing alters the fact that the surprise is paralysing, or at any rate engrossing—all, practically, hang it, that one sees, that one *can* see"(I,168). Seeing, reverberating internally to the spectacle—these are the essence of Strether's experience, and they imply for him a paralysis of sorts; if one is to see with full wondrous appreciation, one can't very well do anything else.

Some such paralysis is implied, I think, by Strether's absorbed rehearsal and mental reenactment of great moments that recur throughout the novel. The fusion (discussed earlier) of past and future tenses that James uses so often to describe Strether's responses serves to release an experience from its immediate bondage to space and time and to allow it to reverberate internally and as long as Strether desires to appreciate it. Strether then possesses his experience forever, but he is equally possessed by it, able to render it, as time goes on, more and more ideal justice, but consequently unable, while cherishing the wonder of his augmenting past, to live in other ways during the present.

Little Bilham seems to embody a similar stance toward experience, and he sheds an interesting light on Strether's earlier outburst in Gloriani's garden: "Didn't you adjure me, in accents I shall never forget, to see, while I've a chance, everything I can?—and *really* to see, for it must have been that only

11. Living in the mind is of course what makes Strether most analogous to the narrator of *The Sacred Fount:* "It would have been almost as embarrassing to have to tell them how little experience I had had in fact as to have had to tell them how much I had had in fancy"(80).

you meant"(I,278). Strether, however, had not urged little Bilham "to see," but rather "to live"; one surely felt at that point in the novel that something more was meant than perception ("—and now I'm old," Strether had recognized, "too old at any rate for what I see"[I,217]). Not "seeing" but "what" he saw was the object of Strether's yearning—the sensuous fulfillment so absent from his own youth.

Later, as the novel begins in its various ways to call this vision into question, an essential shift occurs: the imagined life is gradually replaced by the life of imagination. Strether develops his generous and appreciative vision beyond the point where life can actually meet it, and he abandons life, if it comes to that, rather than his imaginative commitment to that vision. That his vision exceeds the facts is, after all, no reason to discard it, for it has served him well. He has had his youth in the same way that he has had Madame de Vionnet: vicariously, imaginatively, ideally.

Moved by a new vision of life's possibilities, Strether has acted for others in behalf of their youth. His tribute began as vicarious, but gingerly he commenced a new life of his own, with new relations, a new outlook. Inevitably his imagination, embroidering the theme, exceeded reality, and he ends by taking a quiet step in retreat to what is his only acceptable physical role: a slightly chastened but mellow middle-aged observer. His youth, which took place in his imagination, is now over; he has, as it were, "grown up" to himself and regained the age at which he entered the novel. But now, unlike then, he has the right to his fifty-five years, for the blank decades between childhood and middle age have been miraculously redeemed in the past six months. It is not that he has grown older but that he has, finally, matured. He now can confront what they all along have suspected back home—a liaison between Chad Newsome and some French woman—but he confronts it with a perceptive generosity undreamed of in Woollett. And he can do this because the real, "all comically, all tragically"(II,327), has been combined and confused with a romantic vision of supremely civilized human relationships. If Strether's understanding of the combination accounts for his charity, so his understanding of the confusion explains his final, chosen withdrawal.

In the service of that vision he has had his youth, and it is one that can be caressingly perpetuated through memory and imagination, just as it was founded on these faculties. If it is empty of all else, including the shared intimacy and passion of a human relationship, it is because Strether has never, in either of his youths, deeply sought or experienced these things, but rather the vision of them, at first despaired of and now attained. That this is accepted by Strether with wit and poise, that it is enough for him, makes him the most charming imaginative hero in what seems to me James's most perfect work of art and, at the same time, the hero who indicates most clearly the narrow beauty of his creator's vision of life.

VI Fusion and Confusion:
The Golden Bowl

Can wisdom be put in a silver rod?
Or love in a golden bowl?

William Blake, "Thel's Motto"

It struck one for very pity—that they were making a mess of
such charming material; that they were but wasting it and
letting it go. They didn't know how to live—and somehow one
couldn't, if one took an interest in them at all, simply stand
and see it.

The Golden Bowl

THE MOST FRUITFUL CRITICAL APPROACH to a work of art is
not to treat it as, foremost, a problem, and yet I see no other
way of confronting *The Golden Bowl*, which is at once the
most poetic and impenetrable novel of James's career. In my
reading, despite its inferiority to both *The Ambassadors* and
The Wings of the Dove,[1] it stands as his summa. Less perfect

---

1. As F. W. Dupee remarks, "The Turn of the Screw" is James's
small problem child, and *The Golden Bowl* is his large one. Critics
have been magnetically attracted to its polished surface and enigmatic
meaning, though they rarely seem comfortable once they get there and
begin explaining. Personally, I have found Laurence Holland's and Sallie
Sears's readings the most persuasive. Holland makes the best case possible
for a comprehensive, consistently redemptive meaning in the novel, while
Sears, frankly convinced of the book's "moral absurdity," uncovers many
of its endless ambiguities. Maxwell Geismar—less delicately—and Tony
Tanner—less fully—are concerned, like Sears, with the problematic quality

than the former, less compelling than the latter, it nevertheless attempts—unlike anything else he wrote—massively to integrate the requirements of the imagination with "the conditions of life,"[2] to dramatize their fusion. Uniquely, *The Golden Bowl* seems to focus upon the realization, not simply the imagination, of life's possibilities.

The metaphors of expansion in *Roderick Hudson, The Portrait of a Lady, The Ambassadors,* and *The Wings of the Dove* are accordingly transformed into realities. Rowland Mallet has means, Isabel Archer inherits a good deal of money, Milly Theale is born with a fortune; but Adam Verver is mythically wealthy, monetarily one of the giants of the earth. Milly Theale may be a figurative princess, but Maggie Verver is a real one.

---

of the novel. Frederick Crews, Dorothea Krook, Naomi Lebowitz, John Bayley, and Christof Wegelin offer, like Holland, coherent readings of *The Golden Bowl* as a positive and resolved work of art. Finally, most of the better "dissatisfied" criticism is indebted to F. O. Matthiessen's seminal essay in *The Major Phase.* Dupee, *Henry James,* rev. ed. (New York: Dell, 1956), p. 212; Holland, *The Expense of Vision: Essays on the Craft of Henry James* (Princeton, N.J.: Princeton University Press, 1964), pp. 331–407; Sears, *The Negative Imagination: Form and Perception in the Novels of Henry James* (Ithaca, N.Y.: Cornell University Press, 1968), pp. 153–222; Geismar, *Henry James and the Jacobites* (Boston: Houghton Mifflin, 1963), pp. 297–338; Tanner, *"The Golden Bowl,"* London Magazine, n.s., 1 (November 1961), 38–49; Crews, *The Tragedy of Manners: Moral Drama in the Later Fiction of Henry James* (New Haven, Conn.: Yale University Press, 1957), pp. 81–114; Krook, *The Ordeal of Consciousness in Henry James* (New York: Cambridge University Press, 1962), pp. 232–324; Lebowitz, *The Imagination of Loving: Henry James's Legacy to the Novel* (Detroit: Wayne State University Press, 1965), pp. 71–85, 130–142, *passim;* Bayley, *The Characters of Love* (New York: Basic Books, 1961), pp. 203–262; Wegelin, *The Image of Europe in Henry James* (Dallas, Tex.: Southern Methodist University Press, 1955), pp. 122–140; Matthiessen, *Henry James: The Major Phase* (New York: Oxford University Press, 1944), pp. 81–104.

2. The phrase is Flaubert's, quoted approvingly by James in the Preface to *The Golden Bowl* (James, *Art of the Novel,* ed. R. P. Blackmur [New York: Scribner's, 1934], p. 347). Its reference is to the sounded richness requisite of all good prose, and James goes on to claim a responsibility to such "conditions" as the highest of literary goals. I am obviously using the phrase out of context to suggest those areas of life James elsewhere calls "the real"—"the things we cannot possibly *not* know, sooner or later, in one state or another" (*ibid.,* p. 31).

American City, which in another James novel would probably be amusingly situated, by means of inverted commas, as a place existing in the imagination alone—like the "palace of thought" in *The Sacred Fount*—is neither myth nor metaphor in *The Golden Bowl*, but a real city, literally a palace of art, west of the Mississippi and virtually created, it seems, by Adam Verver's awesome fiat.

To be sure, the money—as always in James—creates dilemmas, and the prospect of American City as a future "home" is viewed with horror by Charlotte Verver. Evil and misery are powerfully present within these ostensibly limitless and ideal conditions. But whereas the discovery of the real—the actual, unembroidered conditions of life—occurs late in each of the novels I have so far examined, here it takes place at midpoint. And, rather than occasioning isolation (as with Rowland, Isabel, Maisie, the narrator of *The Sacred Fount*, and Strether), this discovery initiates in Maggie a unique process of development.

In its first phase Maggie's initiation reminds us of Isabel's painful meditative vigil: "Moving for the first time as in the darkening shadow of a false position, she [Maggie] reflected that she should either not have ceased to be right—that is to be confident—or have recognized that she was wrong."[3] We note, however, that "wrong" is not meant as a judgment on Maggie's prior conduct—her relations with her father and her husband—but rather more obscurely refers to the issue of confidence in her position. The word implies recognition of possible problems, but not, as with Isabel, a revaluation of self.

The recognition is itself enough to stimulate Maggie into modes of imagination and discourse well beyond her former

3. James, *The Golden Bowl* (New York: Scribner's 1909), II,6. Subsequent quotations from *The Golden Bowl* refer to this edition (Volumes XXIII and XXIV of the New York Ed.); hereafter, all page references will be included within the text, parenthetically, after the quotation.

timid ways. Like Strether in his late flowering, Maggie moves from passive spectator to the main performer:

Maggie went, she went—she felt herself going; she reminded herself of an actress who had been studying a part and rehearsing it, but who suddenly, on the stage, before the footlights, had begun to improvise . . . It was this very sense of the stage and the footlights that kept her up, made her rise higher; just as it was the sense of action that logically involved some platform—action quite positively for the first time in her life . . . The platform remained for three or four days thus sensibly under her feet, and she had all the while with it the inspiration of quite remarkably, of quite heroically improvising . . . She had but one rule of art—to keep within bounds and not lose her head[II,33].

If this passage begins by reminding us of Strether and "the performance of 'Europe,'" it soon passes into something beyond: the process of living, rendered through the drama metaphor, is in itself essentially a series of scenes, something "that logically involved some platform." What was sophisticated entertainment, an increment of life for Strether, is an all-sustaining, all-encompassing strategy for Maggie. Beyond the capacity of James's other heroes and heroines, she admirably "keeps her head," heroically improvising but always within the bounds of an indelible master script. Through her unrelenting artfulness, Maggie approaches a denouement unique in James's fiction:

She had . . . her back against the door, so that her retreat under his approach must be less than a step, and yet she couldn't for her life . . . have pushed him away. He was so near now that she could touch him, taste him, smell him, kiss him, hold him; he almost pressed upon her, and the warmth of his face . . . was bent upon her with the largeness with which objects loom in dreams. She closed her eyes to it, and so the next instant, against her purpose, had put out her hand, which had met his own and which he held. Then it was that from behind her closed eyes the right word came. "Wait!" It was the word of his own distress and entreaty, the word for both of them, all they had left, their plank now on the great sea: Their hands were locked, and thus she said it again. "Wait. Wait"[II,352–353].

How much this reminds us of the embrace at the end of *The Portrait of a Lady,* and how extraordinarily different it is. There the lover (Caspar Goodwood), threatening Isabel's precarious self-identity and attacking her already strained imaginative commitment to certain forms, is fearfully rejected. Here the lover, deeply committed to the fragile form so long in the making and now near completion, is almost irresistibly desired. There Isabel seems helplessly afloat "in fathomless waters." Suffering Goodwood's kiss, she thinks "of those wrecked and under water following a train of images before they sink." Here "the great sea" of passion encompasses both Maggie and her Prince, and the scene is redolent of her desire for him. Isabel's piercing plea for solitude—"As you love me, as you pity me, leave me alone!"—and her horror of losing herself in the annihilating intimacy urged by Goodwood—these responses contrast directly with Maggie and the Prince's joint decision to "wait." The word seems to issue simultaneously from them both, and it is less a rebuff than a promise, a pledge of the immeasurable intimacy—"the possible, the impossible plash of water"(II,281)—painstakingly sought and now about to be entered upon. The novel, in fact, closes with an all-resolving embrace: "close to her, her face kept before him, his hands holding her shoulders, his whole act enclosing her, he presently echoed: 'See? I see nothing but you.' And the truth of it had with this force . . . so strangely lighted his eyes that as for pity and dread of them she buried her own in his breast" (II,369).

It is only candid to say that an unqualified assent to this conclusion—reversing as it does the deprivation and isolation I have focused on in preceding chapters—would call into question my reading of James. But is it, indeed, an all-resolving embrace? Those words "pity and dread" give us pause, for the phrase touches upon some of the most disturbing ambiguities in the novel, ambiguities that not only qualify the conclusion but render it somewhat appalling. What follows is an attempt to explore the ambiguities behind that final embrace, to determine the significance of this weird affirmation, in *The Golden Bowl,* of the conditions of life.

There were other marble terraces . . . on which he would have known what to think, and would have enjoyed thereby at least the small intellectual fillip of a discerned relation between a given appearance and a taken meaning. The enquiring mind, in these present conditions, might . . . be more sharply challenged; but the result of its attention and its ingenuity, it had unluckily learned to know, was too often to be confronted with a mere dead wall, a lapse of logic, a confirmed bewilderment[I,354–355].

The passage expresses the Prince's mystification at Matcham, but it might equally well refer to the narrator's plight at Newmarch in *The Sacred Fount,* or to the critic's own confusion before the problematic relation between "a given appearance and a taken meaning" in both novels. Appearances stubbornly refuse to become transparent, but tantalizingly sustain conflicting meanings. Any resolution is bound to be ambiguous and shrouded, for the underlying motives of behavior are protected by both James and his "concrete deputy,"[4] Maggie:

She had handed him [the Prince] over to an ignorance that couldn't even try to become indifferent and that yet wouldn't project itself either into the cleared air of conviction. In proportion as he was generous it had bitten into his spirit, and more than once she had said to herself that to break the spell she had cast upon him and that the polished old ivory of her father's inattackable surface made so absolute, he would suddenly commit some mistake or some violence, smash some window-pane for air, fail even of one of his blest inveteracies of taste. In that way, fatally, he would have put himself in the wrong—blighting by a single false step the perfection of his outward show[II, 299].

4. James, *Art of the Novel,* p. 327.

Several motifs here merge. The first is the haunting sense of ignorance that pervades not just the reader but the Prince, Maggie, Charlotte, and—who can tell?—even Adam himself; all must rely on their perceptions alone, on the quality of their interior response to the scene before them. Any journey toward conviction must be made in the imagination; no questions asked are ever satisfactorily answered, and resort to more extreme measures—violence, smashing a "window-pane"—is out of the question. The Prince's "outward show" and the "polished old ivory" of Adam's "inattackable surface" suggest, of course, the figure of the golden bowl itself, internally flawed but superficially, formally intact, the exterior plane on which the action of the novel (but not its meaning) will resolutely take place.

The "spell" cast by Maggie on the Prince and by James on the reader depends upon a certain sustained ignorance, an awakened imagination, and a complete focus on the "outward show," the forms of behavior. The magic transformation thus promised is precarious indeed. But Maggie's spell, if unhindered in its desperate reliance upon silence and surfaces, will end by effecting a metamorphosis from the pretense of a hollow form (the two marriages) to the reality of a redeemed form (Maggie's marriage at the end of the novel), a form filled and thereby fulfilled, made authentic by the painstaking creation of intimacy. The peculiar character of this intimacy and the high cost of attaining it are matters to be later discussed. We need now only observe that the fullest resources of James's late style—with its focus upon the suggestive possibilities of appearances, its reliance upon a character's probing imagination, its refusal to go "behind" and reductively to clarify—are not only used in *The Golden Bowl;* they are what the novel is about.

Behind James's scrupulous respect for surfaces lies a belief that silence is the only adequate medium for expressing real intimacy or passion. Speaking early in the novel of the blows she intuitively realizes that Charlotte has suffered, Maggie tells her father: " 'I wouldn't in any case have let her tell me what would have been dreadful to me. For such wounds and shames *are* dreadful: at least,' she added, catching herself up, 'I suppose they are; for what, as I say, do I know of them? I don't *want* to know!'—she spoke quite with vehemence. 'There are things that are sacred—whether they're joys or pains' " (I,187).

Such fastidious decorum vis-à-vis the "things that are sacred" is omnipresent in James's work. We remember that Isabel had a dislike of going behind curtains, that Strether—in regard to Chad and Madame de Vionnet's intimacy—had all along been trying to suppose nothing. But here the decorum itself becomes a mode of inquiry, one which—through its respect for privacy—can achieve extraordinary results:

Fanny bountifully brooded; there was a point left vague. "And you have it from *him?*—your husband himself has told you?"

" 'Told' me—?"

"Why what you speak of. It isn't of an assurance received from him then that you do speak?"

At which Maggie had continued to stare. "Dear me, no. Do you suppose I've asked him for an assurance?"

"Ah you haven't?" Her companion smiled. "That's what I supposed you might mean. Then, darling, what *have* you—?"

"Asked him for? I've asked him for nothing."

But this in turn made Fanny stare. "Then nothing, that evening of the Embassy dinner, passed between you?"

"On the contrary everything passed."

"Everything—?"

"Everything. I told him what I knew—and I told him how I knew it."

Mrs. Assingham waited. "And that was all?"

"Wasn't it quite enough?"

"Oh love," she bridled, "that's for you to have judged!"

"Then I *have* judged," said Maggie—"I did judge. I made sure he understood—then I left him alone."

Mrs. Assingham wondered. "But he didn't explain—?"

"Explain? Thank God, no!" Maggie threw back her head as

with horror at the thought, then the next moment added: "And I didn't either"[II,214–215].

Maggie wants from the Prince something beyond "explanation"—which would be merely verbal—and to achieve this aim she leaves him alone with his imagination. For it is to this faculty in the Prince she primarily appeals, just as through their imaginations Isabel and Strether are most deeply accessible. Transformation, not explanation, is what Maggie seeks, and poor Fanny Assingham, with her floundering phrases that break off with a dash and a question mark, knows only that the Princess' procedure works at a level outside her own ken.

Beyond these obstacles to an authoritative reading of *The Golden Bowl*—beyond the stress on surfaces and silence and a mode of persuasion that eschews "explaining"—one confronts more disturbing ambiguities, moral confusions that strike a note of absurdity. " 'I think,' " Fanny Assingham says to her husband, referring to the Prince and to Charlotte, " 'there's nothing that they're not now capable of—in their so intense good faith.' 'Good faith?'—he echoed the words, which had in fact something of an odd ring, critically. 'Their false position. It comes to the same thing' "(I,376). This is no simple irony directed with sarcasm against Charlotte and the Prince; "good faith" and "false position" exist in no simple-minded, ironic equation. Rather, it is genuine good faith, the bond that makes them, in Fanny's ominous word, so "capable."

Everyone's faith has been good, none better than Maggie's. Yet Fanny tells her husband, "Well, she [Maggie] did it originally—she *began* the vicious circle. For that—though you make round eyes at my associating her with 'vice'—is simply what it has been. It's their mutual consideration, all round, that has made it the bottomless gulf; and they're really so embroiled but because, in their way, they've been so improbably *good* . . . Before she knew it, at any rate, her little scruples and her little lucidities, which were really so divinely blind—her feverish little sense of justice, as I say—had brought the two others together as her grossest misconduct couldn't have done"(I,394,396).

Here again, to the extent that we believe at all in the different facets of the relationships before us, the irony is multiple. "Scruples" and "lucidities" have the effect of "grossest misconduct"—all four characters are simultaneously innocent and guilty—and one of the most astute critics of the novel, Sallie Sears, accordingly declares: "The terms 'good' and 'evil' in such a context lose their meaning, become interchangeable and therefore in an ultimate sense 'absurd.' And morally this book is absurd."[5] But Mrs. Sears's conclusion, perhaps inherent in the premises of the novel, is not borne out by its development. Instead, we perceive a latent but gradually expanding critique of the liaison between Charlotte and the Prince, along with a sustained, though equally latent, celebration of Maggie's odyssey into experience. Before analyzing such developments, however, let us examine the given, "unreconstructed" situation of the novel: the flawed raw materials visible everywhere in Book I, the corrupt situation that Maggie must confront and redeem if her "spell" and its results are ultimately to persuade us.

"You're at any rate a part of his collection," Maggie tells the Prince early in the novel, "one of the things that can only be got over here. You're a rarity, an object of beauty, an object of price"(I,12). People used as things—collected, manipulated, exploited: this has been the cardinal evil in the Jamesian world since *Roderick Hudson,* and one wants to know the tone in which Maggie speaks these words. Is she playfully mocking the vocabulary of acquisition, or does she uncritically assent

5. Sears, *Negative Imagination,* p. 222. Mrs. Sears's study did not appear until my own manuscript was well under way, but her finest chapter deals with *The Golden Bowl,* the only novel on which I had not yet begun to write. Consequently I have benefited from her in preparing this essay. Our interest in James has several points in common, but our methods of criticism, and the conclusions we reach, are essentially different.

to it? Is she less intelligent than we are led to believe, or merely less naïve? In any case, in Book II of the novel Maggie begins to open her eyes, as she recognizes "that it had been for all the world as if Charlotte had been 'had in,' as the servants always said of extra help, because they had thus suffered it to be pointed out to them that if their family coach lumbered and stuck the fault was in its lacking its complement of wheels. Having but three . . . it had wanted another, and what had Charlotte done from the first but begin to act, on the spot, and ever so smoothly and beautifully, as a fourth?" (II,23).

The reader looks in vain, in this paragraph and its neighbors, for some slight expression of self-indictment or recoil in Maggie's response to this recognition. "Isabel's cheek burned," James tells us, when she discovered the mixture of motives in her marriage to Osmond. One would settle for less than burning cheeks in *The Golden Bowl*, but what Maggie experiences—instead of any moral recriminations, however nuanced—is "a repeated challenge" in the image of "Amerigo and Charlotte . . . pulling [the coach] while she and her father were not so much as pushing" (II,23).

There are other examples of manipulation that one might cite, but surely the most powerful instance in the novel—indeed the most powerful in James's *oeuvre*—is the passage about the infamous "silken halter" that Adam seems to hold about Charlotte's neck: "the likeness of their connexion wouldn't have been wrongly figured if he had been thought of as holding in one of his pocketed hands the end of a long silken halter looped around her beautiful neck. He didn't twitch it, yet it was there; he didn't drag her, but she came." Maggie then translates Adam's enigmatic smile as follows:

"Yes, you see—I lead her now by the neck, I lead her to her doom, and she doesn't so much as know what it is, though she has a fear in her heart which, if you had the chances to apply your ear there that I, as a husband, have, you would hear thump and thump and thump. She thinks it *may* be, her doom,

175

the awful place over there—awful for *her;* but she's afraid to ask, don't you see? just as she's afraid of not asking; just as she's afraid of so many other things that she sees multiplied all about her now as perils and portents. She'll know, however—when she does know"[II,287–288].

In his balanced essay on the novel, Walter Wright claims that this passage does not offer "objective evidence of Adam's callousness. The images show rather Maggie's awakening pity" toward Charlotte.[6] Such a reading (indeed any reading that attempts to "defuse" the passage) creates its own problems: for one thing, "the likeness of their connexion would not have been wrongly figured" sounds very much like impersonal and objective narration. For another—and more important—the cruelty in the scene can be adroitly shifted about in any number of readings, but it cannot be made to disappear. Maggie does express sympathy toward Charlotte's plight, to be sure; nevertheless, this horrifying vision of Adam is either accurate, in which case he is something of a monster, or it is only Maggie's subjective view of him. In either case, her failure to reassess her father, to reexamine her relationship with him, must be seen as appalling.

Exploitation, then, is rampant in the human relations depicted in *The Golden Bowl,* and marriage is the deeply flawed form which it undermines. Maggie's triumph, if it is to convince us, must be free of such manipulation before it can possibly redeem the hollow marriages of Book I. The closer one looks (beginning with Adam), the more enormous the task appears.

Adam's first wife having been, "in the strange scheme of things, so promptly removed"(I,143), he is now confronted with a new set of problems; the Mrs. Rances and the Mrs. Lutches are upon him, and he soon becomes aware of "his own special deficiency, his unfortunate lack of a wife to whom applications could be referred"(I,151).

6. Walter F. Wright, "Maggie Verver: Neither Saint nor Witch," *Nineteenth-Century Fiction,* 12 (June 1957), 59–71.

The need for a secretary-wife increases dramatically when his daughter marries. Maggie herself says: "It was as if you couldn't be in the market when you were married to *me*. Or rather as if I kept people off, innocently, by being married to you. Now that I'm married to someone else you're, as in consequence, married to nobody. Therefore you may be married to anybody, to everybody. People don't see why you shouldn't be married to *them*" (I,172).

The passage is charming, but Maggie's speaking playfully of their relationship in terms of "marriage" points toward the deepest ambiguity in the novel: James's handling of the father-daughter connection. Treated throughout with a reverent and expansive tenderness, this connection relentlessly impinges upon and distorts those others that surround it. Adam's giving Maggie a husband creates Maggie's need to find Adam a wife; and, sensing this concern in his daughter, Adam rises to the occasion:

Once he had recognized it there everything became coherent. The sharp point to which all his light converged was that the whole call of his future would be in his so managing that Maggie would less and less appear to herself to have forsaken him . . . The way . . . to put her [Maggie] at peace was to provide for his future—that is for hers—by marriage, by a marriage as good . . . as hers had been . . . He had seen that Charlotte could contribute—what he hadn't seen was what she could contribute *to*. When it had all supremely cleared up and he had simply settled this service to his daughter well before him as the proper direction of his young friend's leisure, the cool darkness had again closed round him, but his moral lucidity was constituted . . . To think of it merely for himself would have been . . . even as he had just lately felt, even doing all justice to that condition—yes, impossible. But there was a grand difference in thinking of it for his child[I,207–209].

One may recognize the "good faith" and benevolence in this passage and still find it deeply perverse. And perhaps the locus of the perversity is simply in Adam's feeling that "he had seen that Charlotte could contribute." The verb is inhuman, or rather it bypasses the strictly human—the uniqueness of Charlotte Stant—and focuses instead upon the various things she is good for. As with his original epiphany—when he discovered in himself the collector's passion—Adam's illumination in this scene is obscurely artistic. Using human materials, he intends to reassure Maggie by creating a grand design of interconnected marriages: this is "what she could contribute *to*." Serenely deciding that a "service to his daughter" is what best becomes "his young friend's leisure," Adam unhesitatingly prepares to move centrally into Charlotte Stant's life, having considered everything except whether he loves her or not.

Marriage, one realizes, does not entail a sacred relationship for Adam; it certainly did not as far as the former Mrs. Verver was concerned, and, as to the future one, it is proposed as a "proper direction" for "her leisure." The deep, almost religious emotion of the passage has little to do with Charlotte save as contributory agent. Its real sources are his "service to his daughter" and the crystalization of his own imaginative, artistic design. Like Isabel, he needs to see a meaning or a value beyond his partner—and this is of course to make *use* of the partner—before he can see her at all.

Charlotte is not slow to grasp the limitations in such an arrangement. Part II ends with her deciding to marry Adam, and Part III opens with her waiting at the party "to be rejoined by her companion, who . . . would know where to find her"(I,245). We discover this companion to be not the man she has just married, as it were, on the preceding page, but the Prince instead. Her own husband has, as usual, chosen not to accompany her to the party; the Prince's wife has, as usual, left him in order to visit in private with her father. There is, consequently, a good deal of truth, as well as oversimplification and ominous flippancy, in Charlotte's comment to Fanny Assingham: "I've simply to see the truth of the matter—see that Maggie thinks more on the whole of fathers than of husbands"(I,257).

Against this cynical conception of the marriages in Book I we need to place Maggie's naïve view, brought to consciousness by her discovery of the "pagoda" in her life:

The pagoda in her blooming garden figured the arrangement— how otherwise was it to be named?—by which, so strikingly, she had been able to marry without breaking, as she liked to put it, with her past. She had surrendered herself to her husband without the shadow of a reserve or a condition and yet she hadn't all the while given up her father by the least little inch[II,5].

Without caviling, one notices that Maggie's thoughts strain credibility. We needn't accept Charlotte's cynical formulation in order to be puzzled at Maggie's conviction of having utterly surrendered herself to her husband without losing anything of her relationship with Adam. More to the point, what kind of unconditional intimacy could she have with the Prince and yet not know that he was bored, that he was having an affair with her stepmother? Such questions about the nature of Maggie's former intimacy with the Prince round out my critique of the marriages in Book I. We can now take a longer look at her development in Book II and at the transformation she undergoes in seeking a new intimacy with her husband. For in the second half of the novel James leisurely unfolds both the drama of the Princess' awakening and the effect of that awakening on the rife exploitation and the flawed marriages within which she has been blithely living.

Maggie's first impression is of frustration and smallness. By contrast, the lavishly artful pagoda, rising "far aloft" before her with "apertures and outlooks," suggests the elevated condition of knowledge and experience. The reader imagines Charlotte and the Prince high within the pagoda, peering down

179

on Maggie who "quite helplessly" scans the elevation, and this literally occurs later, as Maggie and Adam, returning from the Park, look up and find the other two "perched together in the balcony . . . gay . . . amused . . . [looking like] truly superior beings"(II,98–99). One remembers Strether's yearning to join little Bilham on the balcony, the vantage point of genuine initiation into the Parisian scene.

Undaunted, Maggie quietly presses on, but she finds her husband and Charlotte mystifyingly a step ahead of her and smoothing the way:

> It was a worked-out scheme for their not wounding her, for their behaving to her quite nobly; to which each had in some winning way induced the other to contribute, and which therefore . . . proved that she had become with them a subject of intimate study . . . They had built her in with their purpose— which was why, above her, a vault seemed more heavily to arch; so that she sat there . . . as in a bath of benevolence artfully prepared for her, over the brim of which she could but just manage to see by stretching her neck. Baths of benevolence were very well, but at least, unless one were a patient of some sort, a nervous eccentric or a lost child, one wasn't usually so immersed save by one's request. It wasn't in the least what *she* had requested [II,43–44].

"Contribute," "built her in," "subject of study," a "worked-out scheme," an arching vault—this vocabulary used to express an ostensibly intimate relationship reminds us of Adam's plan for Charlotte, and what they have in common is a great deal of skillful manipulation. So treated as a child, Maggie feels helplessly outmaneuvered. Their artfully built and enigmatic vault, like the pagoda, arches oppressively above. Being studied and considered as a patient is quite vexing and demeaning, Maggie feels. Yet one of the major ironies of *The Golden Bowl* consists of her own behavior during Book II, as the Princess ferociously studies and "deals with" the three people most intimately related to her, reducing their manipulative skills, by comparison, to mere child's play.

In dealing with her husband on the new basis, the first challenge she confronts is the Prince's irresistible embrace: "She gave up, let her idea go, let everything go; her one consciousness was that he was taking her again into his arms. It was not till afterwards that she discriminated as to this; felt how the act operated with him *instead* of the words he hadn't uttered—operated in his view as probably better than any words, as always better in fact at any time than anything"(II,28–29).

As early as *Roderick Hudson,* I have suggested, James's fiction displays recurrent patterns of imagery for "holding on," keeping control. Failure to hold on to his genius leads to Roderick's fatal dissipation; Isabel's recurrent temptation is to "let go"—either by hissing an insult at Madame Merle or surrendering to Caspar Goodwood's embrace. As always in James, the embrace itself is a covertly sinister challenge to the heroine's selfhood; one need only consider *The Portrait of a Lady, The Bostonians,* and *What Maisie Knew.* The intimacy and loss of control it invokes is terrifying to Maggie. "She tasted of a sort of terror of the weakness [it] produced in her"(II,29), as the Prince threatens that tiny kernel of an idea by means of which alone she can find her way. A few pages later the threat recurs: "Yes, she was in his exerted grasp . . . but she was at the same time in the grasp of her conceived responsibility, and the extraordinary thing was that of the two intensities the second was presently to become the sharper . . . Strange enough was this sense for her . . . of possessing, by miraculous help, some advantage that . . . she might either give up or keep . . . And what her husband's grasp really meant . . . was that she *should* give it up: it was exactly for this that he had resorted to unfailing magic" (II,56).

Although the Prince's embrace challenges Maggie's moral integrity and is felt as an overwhelming and "unfailing magic," her own swift-moving mind and fired imagination constitute in themselves another kind of magic, a "miraculous help." She opposes her husband's sensuous expertise with her own mental agility and grace. Such talents finally exert the greater attraction, and we might now take a closer look at Maggie's magic in operation.

Learning with a thrill to play the sophisticated game of "squaring" those who would "square" her, to use the language of *What Maisie Knew,* Maggie begins intensely to live. And, while her transformation constitutes the "act of life" in the novel, it is most revealingly described, again and again, as the consummate manipulative skill of the artist:

They might have been—really charming as they showed in the beautiful room [during the game of bridge] . . . figures rehearsing some play of which she herself was the author . . . They might in short have represented any mystery they would; the point being predominantly that the key to the mystery, the key that could wind and unwind it without a snap of the spring, was there in her pocket . . . she passed round the house and looked into the drawing-room, lighted also, but empty now, and seeming to speak the more in its own voice of all the possibilities she controlled. Spacious and splendid, like a stage again awaiting a drama, it was a scene she might people, by the press of her spring, either with serenities and dignities and decencies, or with terrors and shames and ruins, things as ugly as those formless fragments of her golden bowl she was trying so hard to pick up[II,235–236].

Coming into life means transforming life into a fully self-conscious art in which the destinies of others are, with splendid benevolence, both perceived and controlled. Maggie finally combines, as it were, Chad's effectiveness at living with Strether's artistic imagination. Unlike those former "palaces of thought"—lovingly erected by Rowland, Isabel, Maisie, the narrator of *The Fount* and Strether—which were inevitably doomed to collapse, the "fragments of her golden bowl" are so tenaciously put together by Maggie that she contrives, by the end of the novel, an edifice whose potent magic competes with and annihilates the hitherto oppressive pagoda: Charlotte and Adam depart below, and the Princess—with the Prince at her side—holds unchallenged possession of the balcony (II,363). She has a fully commanding view; from her eminence she now can see everything.

But surely this triumphant edifice is itself suspect. Those other "palaces of thought" did not collapse through pure fortuitousness; they were founded on illusions, albeit generous ones, and they were constructed, in part, through exploitation and manipulation of others. There is in fact something appalling in the uncritical use of the author's relation to his characters as a model for Maggie's relation to her family. Such exultant control of "all the possibilities" is never attained in Jame's prior novels, and Tony Tanner, among other critics, indicates the sinister quality in Maggie's artful development: "The pathetically inept performer grows into the relentless author. At the time of that crucial card game she is thrilled 'with the idea of the prodigious effect she had at her command.' Maggie's 'revenge'—the word is, tellingly, used only once—is not a matter of a sharp knife and a dark alley: it lies in her 'compassionate patronage.' Her revenge is in saving them—on her own terms."[7]

Though Tanner puts his finger on the perversity, he perhaps undervalues the beauty and weird sincerity of Maggie's plan, the passion with which James could invest her imaginative concern for "serenities and dignities and decencies," for the forms in life. The Princess' speculation continues:

. . . she saw as in a picture . . . why it was she had been able to give herself from the first so little to the vulgar heat of her wrong. She might fairly . . . have missed it as a lost thing; have yearned . . . for the straight vindictive view, the rights of resentment, the rages of jealousy, the protests of passion . . . a range of feelings which for many women would have meant so much, but which for *her* husband's wife, for her father's daughter, figured nothing nearer to experience than a wild eastern caravan,

7. Tanner, *"Golden Bowl,"* p. 43.

looming into view with crude colours in the sun, fierce pipes
in the air, high spears against the sky, all a thrill, a natural
joy to mingle with, but turning off short before it reached her
and plunging into other defiles[II,236–237].

Like Isabel, Maggie eschews "the straight vindictive view,"
the temptation to let go and sound off. Such a conventional,
vulgar range of feeling is conveyed by the figure of "a wild
eastern caravan," the same figure James used in the Preface
to *The Portrait of a Lady* to describe the less interesting kinds
of action found in many novels but not in his. Instead Maggie
takes a higher course that soars beyond the "thrill" and "natural joy" of any release, any expression of outrage.

The resultant strains and sublimations thus imposed—on
Maggie, on the forms of social intercourse, on the novel—become unbearable, and behind the Princess' intended generosity
one occasionally hears quite other accents:

It was in fact as if, thanks to her hovering image of him [the
Prince] confronted with this admirable creature [Charlotte] even
as she was confronted, there glowed upon her from afar . . . a
deep explanatory light . . . He had given her something to con-
form to, and she hadn't unintelligently . . . "gone back on"
him . . . by not conforming. They were together thus, he and
she, close, close together—whereas Charlotte, though rising there
radiantly before her, was really off in some darkness of space
that would steep her in solitude and harass her with care. The
heart of the Princess swelled accordingly even in her abasement . . . [II,250].

It is a curious intimacy Maggie exults in, one which consists
more in the exclusion of Charlotte than closeness with the
Prince. If Maggie's swelling heart does not betoken revenge,
it is still far short of charity; Charlotte is beginning to suffer
the isolation that Maggie has known so well, and the Princess
perhaps takes a grain of pleasure in enumerating the anxieties
that await her stepmother. Later Maggie refers to her as

"poor Charlotte," imagining in clear detail "the chill" of the "stiffest admonition" administered by the Prince to Charlotte: "It was positive in the Princess that for this she breathed Charlotte's cold air—turned away from him in it with her, turned with her, in growing compassion, this way and that, hovered behind her . . . Marvellous the manner in which, under such imaginations, Maggie thus circled and lingered—quite as if she were, materially, following her unseen, counting every step she helplessly wasted, noting every hindrance that brought her to a pause"(II,282–283).

Such compassion is somewhat ambiguous. Maggie lingers over the pain her stepmother is feeling, and, like a huntress, her imagination hovers, circles, follows, counts, notes. This is a vocabulary we have repeatedly encountered in James—most conspicuously in *The Sacred Fount*. There it indicated the narrator's exploitative-sacrificial stance toward the other characters, and here too we feel both motives at work, not merely the explicit one of selfless compassion. The problem, of course, is that nowhere does Maggie recognize the darker side of her behavior, just as in the caravan passage quoted earlier, she never sees more than the "wrong" done to her and her own subsequent magnanimity.

Repressed resentment seems to play a larger role in Maggie's second "reconciliation" scene with Charlotte. Knowing that Charlotte is desperate, the Princess exaggeratedly assumes her former posture as "the poor little person." But within, "in a secret, responsive ecstasy," she wonders "if there weren't some supreme abjection with which she might be inspired"(II,313). She manages finally to offer Charlotte a pretense of victory, confessing to her own "failure." This emphasis on abject groveling ("But why wasn't it still left to push further and, from the point of view of personal pride, grovel lower?"[II,329]) is disturbing in its suggestion of obscure and perverse self-gratification. Further, if Maggie is convinced that Charlotte no longer believes her ignorant, then the entire scene becomes an elaborate charade, in which, as Sallie Sears declares, Maggie offers "the ambiguous charity of allowing her to save face, while having to know that she is being so allowed." And, with only slight oversimplification, Mrs. Sears calls the scene "a *tour de force* of masochistic self-manipulation and disguised sadism."[8]

From this wide range of motives—some admirable, some appalling—Maggie draws the energy to enter into and gain mastery over "the conditions of life." Nowhere do we see this mastery more clearly displayed than at the smashing of the golden bowl. Like a released genie the Prince enters the room. Without uttering a word, Maggie picks up the pieces, giving her husband time to collect himself enough to see what she is offering him:

. . . the possibility, richer with every lapsing moment, that her husband would have . . . a new need of her . . . It struck her truly as so new that he would . . . be *really* needing her for the first time in their whole connexion. No, he had used her, he had even exceedingly enjoyed her, before this; but there had been no precedent for that character of a proved necessity to him which she was rapidly taking on . . . It had operated within her now to the last intensity, her glimpse of the precious truth that by her helping him, helping him to help himself, as it were, she should help him to help *her*. Hadn't she fairly got into his labyrinth with him? . . . "Yes look, look," she seemed to see him hear her say even while her sounded words were other— "look, look, both at the truth that still survives in that smashed evidence and at the even more remarkable appearance that I'm not such a fool as you supposed me. Look at the possibility that, since I *am* different there may still be something in it for you—if you're capable of working with me to get that out. Consider of course as you must the question of what you may have to surrender, on your side, what price you may have to pay, whom you may have to pay *with*, to set this advantage free; but take in at any rate that there *is* something for you if you don't too blindly spoil your chance for it"[II,186–188].

In this great breakthrough scene, unique in James, Maggie

8. Sears, *Negative Imagination*, pp. 221, 219.

makes her bid. Displacing Charlotte and the pagoda, she begins to enter the Prince's labyrinth with him. But the intimacy mutely proposed, we are bound to notice, has little to do with shared affection; it is rather a joining of separate needs. More than mere "use" and "enjoyment," such need is still far from that radical "necessity" of a man and woman who share a relationship vital to both their lives; it is, instead, the more pragmatic "necessity" of two people, each in desperate straits, who can solve their separate problems only by solving them together. Less an emotional plea than a cool and intelligent proposition is what we hear in Maggie's repeated "look, look" and "there may be still something in it for you." Prices, advantages, other people as the currency used, chances that may be spoiled—it is all pragmatic, shrewd, detached, disturbingly close to a business deal.

The Prince accepts the gambit and gradually abandons Charlotte as the price of his own "salvation." In fact, he so fully accedes to Maggie's magic that, by the end of the novel, she wonders if an opposite problem has arisen:

She had begun . . . by asking herself how she could make him think more of her; but what was it after all he was thinking now? He kept his eyes on her telegram; he read it more than once, easy as it was . . . to understand; during which she found herself almost awestruck with yearning, almost on the point of marking somehow what she had marked in the garden at Fawns with Charlotte—that she had truly come unarmed. She didn't bristle with intentions . . . She had nothing but her old idea, the old one he knew; she hadn't the ghost of another. Presently in fact, when four or five minutes had elapsed, it was as if she positively hadn't so much even as that one. He gave her back her paper, asking with it if there were anything in particular she wished him to do[II,339].

Maggie has certainly succeeded with her husband, and in this scene it is as though, hypnotized by her, he cannot emerge from his dazed state. His wife—no longer fallible—has become a dazzling and formidable creature. He does not pretend to fathom her intentions; she will forever "bristle" with them, enchanting precisely at the expense of shared familiarity. His expectation of her myriad intentions prevents intimacy between them, and Maggie wishes she could convey her "unarmed" state with him as she did in the garden with Charlotte. The comparison is provocative as we remember the ambiguous mixture of compassion and sadism at work in that scene.

She fails, at any rate, to appear disarmed, and, with humble acceptance of ignorance on his part and authority on hers, the Prince asks if there is anything in particular she wishes him to do. Captivated, he has eyes only for his wife, and such success is, in its way, a stunning achievement for Maggie. The larger conceptual significance of this achievement and its peculiar liabilities are the last considerations in our analysis of *The Golden Bowl.*

Midway in the novel Fanny Assingham begins to confront the implications of her own well-intentioned meddling in the affairs of the Ververs, and she has a tear-filled scene with her husband, suspecting the anguish that is imminent. Through the sympathy he displays at "this small crisis" and through their facing together "the depths" of the situation, Fanny manages to come up with the only possible basis for salvation: "What was the basis, which Fanny absolutely exacted, but that Charlotte and the Prince must be saved—so far as consistently speaking of them as still safe might save them?"(I,378).

Laurence Holland has perceptively focused on this passage as an indication of the novel's most pressing concerns: "The process of forging a marriage in which no breach shows because none exists virtually requires the lie which James's mannered style creates: the pretence that any 'weak spot,' any division in the past or any impending breach, does not exist by making certain that it does not show. The marriages can *become* true only by pretending that they are so *already*. Only by gilding the bowl—by consistently speaking as if the characters and marriages were still safe, by giving form to ignorance, blindness, projected faith as well as to knowledge and insight—can the novel appreciate what is given even in the flawed or fragmented remnants, and restore their promise by transforming and making good on it."[9]

Holland's account seems to me completely persuasive as a reading of James's intent in *The Golden Bowl* (though not of the book's final effect). Moreover it indicates how the novel celebrates life by simultaneously celebrating art. That is, to "make good" on the promise of life, it must rely on the pretence of art: it professes an absolute good faith in its own forms and surfaces; it protectively screens out confessions and revelation; it keeps spoken speculation on the outer form of the bowl, while patiently working at the flaw, as it were, unseen and from within. In its use of screens and ambiguous forms, the novel is a massive reworking of *The Sacred Fount*, with this reversal at the end: the painstakingly constructed form finally holds the promise of intimacy, does not collapse in the hero's face. Something like this fusion of structural design and personal goal seems implied by Maggie's words, late in the novel, to Fanny Assingham:

"I want a happiness without a hole in it big enough for you to poke in your finger."

"A brilliant perfect surface—to begin with at least. I see."

"The golden bowl—as it *was* to have been." And Maggie dwelt musingly on this obscured figure. "The bowl with all our happiness in it. The bowl without the crack"[II,216–217].

By the close of the novel Maggie seems magically to have achieved just such a restitution of the old forms. She has played the naïve little girl with Charlotte—as in the past she really

9. Holland, *Expense of Vision*, p. 387.

was—and she now proposes to her husband an even more audacious recovery of the past, as she plans their last evening with Adam and Charlotte:

"But there's always also the chance of his proposing to me that *we* shall have our last hours together; I mean that he and I shall. He may wish to take me off to dine with him somewhere alone—and do it in memory of old days. I mean," the Princess went on, "the *real* old days before my grand husband was invented and, much more, before his grand wife was . . . In that case he'll leave you Charlotte to take care of in our absence. You'll have to carry *her* off somewhere for your last evening; unless you may prefer to spend it with her here. I shall then see that you dine, that you have everything, quite beautifully. You'll be able to do as you like"[II,343].

One actually feels Maggie skillfully testing the golden bowl of her newly forged happiness against all the pressures, now overcome, that originally caused its flaws: the pointed division (*"we"*) into the original couples, the serene rejoicing in the "old days," the rich emphasis on "invented" as descriptive of the Prince and Charlotte, the word conveying both their original purchase as husband and wife and their more recently created new identities, shaped by Maggie's unfailing energy. Even more bristling are Maggie's pregnant references to Charlotte and the Prince together: "carry *her* off . . . your last evening . . . You'll be able to do as you like." Loaded as these phrases once were, they have now become innocent, no longer the pretence of innocence but the real thing, achieved through the redemptive process of Maggie's magic. The high cost of such a process, the questionable changes it brings about, and the curious quality of the intimacy it promises—a discussion of these liabilities is at last in order and will bring this chapter to a close.

"He did it for *me,* he did it for me," she moaned, "he did it . . . that our freedom—meaning, beloved man, simply and solely mine—should be greater instead of less; he did it . . . to

liberate me so far as possible from caring what became of him."
. . . Thus she felt the whole weight of their case drop afresh
upon her shoulders, was confronted . . . with the prime source
of her haunted state. It all came from her not having been able
not to mind—not to mind what became of him; not having been
able, without anxiety, to let him go his way and take his risk
and lead his life[II,81].

If the first half of this recognition recalls Isabel's mixed feelings about Ralph's generous gift, the second half goes even
further: Maggie discerns her stubborn refusal to let her father
"go his own way." Many critics of the novel, impressed with
Maggie's insight in this passage, have gone on to praise her
comprehensively in terms of a consistent growth into mature
self-awareness. Christof Wegelin, one of the most astute
Jamesian critics, writes:

[The point] is above all that part of her knowledge is of her
own innocent complicity, for she learns that her own ignorance . . . has been a necessary condition of the evil which to
her horror she comes to find "seated all at its ease" where she
has "dreamed only of good." Her tender relation with her father
has been part of that innocence, and the crucial result of her
new wisdom, the sign also of its great personal cost to her, is
the fact that at the end she accepts her separation from him,
realizing that she can indeed *not* have the cake and eat it too,
that if her marriage is to be the emotional reality which alone
will compel the Prince, she must give up the father who has
conceived it as the mere acquisition of another treasure.[10]

One would like to assent to this view of the novel—if only
the rest of *The Golden Bowl* supported it. For if Maggie "realizes" everything—about her marriage, about emotional reality,
about her father, about acquisition and treasure—that Wegelin
credits to her, then surely there should be abundant passages
that express such realizations. Instead, a good deal *after* this
passage, we see Maggie—with unconscious egotism—speak to

10. Wegelin, *Image of Europe*, pp. 125–126.

Fanny about Adam's "good faith" as "his faith in [Charlotte's] taking almost as much interest in me as he himself took." When Fanny responds that "he'll never have shown that he expected of her a quarter as much as she must have understood he was to give"(II,174–175), we vainly wait for Maggie to ask, simply, "give to whom?" For his deepest interest and affection remain reserved for his daughter alone; lacking these, Charlotte lacks a husband, regardless of the fortune she has been given. As a unique human being rather than an extremely useful and talented woman drafted into a difficult situation, Charlotte often seems hardly to exist for Maggie. Nor can she envisage her father as in any sense culpable.

> "For they're the ones who are saved," she went on. "We're the ones who are lost."
> "Lost—?"
> "Lost to each other—father and I." And then as her friend [Fanny] appeared to demur, "Oh yes," Maggie quite lucidly declared, "lost to each other really much more than Amerigo and Charlotte are; since for them it's just, it's right, it's deserved, while for us it's only sad and strange and not caused by our fault"[II,333].

Wegelin notwithstanding, these are not the remarks of a woman who has "realized" anything about the insidious link between her relationship with her father, her relationship with her husband, and Charlotte's relationship with both men. The soft, self-pitying tone verges on fatuousness in the neatness of its black and white distinctions, in its lack of self-perception. Occurring only thirty-six pages before the novel closes, this speech casts into permanent obscurity the meaning of Maggie's development.

Moreover, the intimacy finally attained may disturb the reader as much as the lack of it originally did. From nobody Maggie has become everything for the Prince; her magic has mesmerized him, and we see him do little but brood and follow directions in the latter half of the novel. He is "hers" indeed, he sees nothing else, and the self-loss implied in such adoration—which partly accounts for Maggie's final feeling of "pity and dread"—seems out of place in a marriage relationship, seems more appropriate in the worship of a goddess. For this is what Maggie has become, the goddess in the Prince's world, and resolution though it be, it is still devoid of a shared or balanced intimacy.

Finally, what are the costs of this ambiguous triumph? Heretofore the requirements of the imagination and the unadorned conditions of life have been mutually incompatible in the Jamesian world, and the payment exacted for their fusion in *The Golden Bowl* may well be beyond the reader's tolerance. The unrelenting protective opacity of the prose, the artifice of manners "refined beyond the point of civilization,"[11] the novel's refusal to render Adam's point of view when it is needed most, its selective punishment of Charlotte, Maggie's inability to see what is disturbing in her relationship with her father, what has been inadequate in the one with her husband—all of these factors simultaneously trouble the reader and permit the novel's resolution: the remaking of the golden bowl, the imaginative transformation of experience.

One feels, at the end, the enormous contrivance and manipulation of human relationships in the book; Maggie's awakened imagination has a field day indeed. But the experience on which it is working, the marriage it is salvaging, the intimacy it is seeking involve modes of behavior—deceiving, exploiting, concealing—that are neither redeemed nor critically rendered, but rather, I think, sidestepped. When Adam's interest in Charlotte is compared to his collector's instinct, the narrator tells us that "Nothing perhaps might affect us as queerer, had we time to look into it, than this application of the same measure of value to such different pieces of property as old Persian carpets, say, and new human acquisitions"(I,196). It is indeed queer,

---

11. T. S. Eliot, "On Henry James," in *The Question of Henry James: A Collection of Critical Essays,* ed. F. W. Dupee (New York: Holt, 1945), p. 113. Eliot uses this acid phrase to describe the Boston society of the turn of the century that he and James both knew so well.

and, in a novel of such length and of such focus on just this problem, we wish that James would take the "time to look into it" a little further. But the book is only a quarter completed at this passage; not until the final pages does such an attitude on James's part genuinely vex us:

The two noble persons seated in conversation and at tea fell thus into the splendid effect and the general harmony: Mrs. Verver and the Prince fairly "placed" themselves, however unwittingly, as high expressions of the kind of human furniture required aesthetically by such a scene. The fusion of their presence with the decorative elements, their contribution to the triumph of selection, was complete and admirable; though to a lingering view, a view more penetrating than the occasion really demanded, they also might have figured as concrete attestations of a rare power of purchase[II,360].

A view more penetrating than the occasion really demanded—this coyness, or unwillingness, or confusion is what most grates. In *The Sacred Fount* the refusal to clarify was annoying but cogent; here, where so much more seems at stake, where the exploitation is less murky and more appalling, it is disastrous. For this morally dubious world thus unassessed and accepted is close, indeed, to the world finally recognized in James's fiction from *Roderick Hudson* on, recognized and rejected as uninhabitable.

Maggie and the Prince come together, they assent to life; but in his perversely brilliant way, consciously or unconsciously, James renders to the full the intolerable price to be paid. He may ostensibly "worship" the conditions of life, of human passion and intimacy, but at a deeper level he doesn't seem particularly to like them. And this makes for the peculiar ambiguity—the combination of ostensible assent and implicit rejection—in James's work that this book has set out to explore: his paradoxical rendering of human experience and the various enriching and isolating stances the imagination takes toward it.

Conclusion

We must grant the artist his subject, his idea, his donnée; *our criticism is applied only to what he makes of it.*

> Henry James, *"The Art of Fiction"*

A man writes as he can; but those who use his writings have the further responsibility of redefining their scope, an operation . . . which alone uses them to the full.

> R. P. Blackmur, *"A Critic's Job of Work"*

WHEN A FEMALE ACQUAINTANCE of James was once foolish enough to ask him the meaning of a certain passage in *The Wings of the Dove,* she received, it is alleged, this reply: " 'My dear lady,' Mr. James said coldly, 'if after the infinite labour I give to my literature I am unable to convey to you my meaning, how can you expect me to do so by mere word of mouth?' "[1] Bearing in mind certain distinctions between a modest work of criticism and a creative masterpiece, I should like, nevertheless, to invoke this mot of James in regard to the conclusion of my argument: the main points have either been made or they have not, and what follows is less an ultimate attempt to "convey to you my meaning" than a summary of some essentials.

1. Quoted from Simon Nowell-Smith, *The Legend of the Master: Henry James* (London: Constable, 1947), p. 111.

I can perhaps best begin by counterpointing my view of the life in James's fiction with Leon Edel's view of the life of the novelist. In the Introduction to his massive biography, Edel is quick to address himself to what he recognizes as a focal problem in Jamesian criticism: "the belief that there was, so to speak, no 'life' behind the Art of Henry James, that his was a purely cerebrating genius."[2] With four more projected volumes in mind, Edel vigorously dissents from this view, and he asks the rhetorical question: was James actually like John Marcher in "The Beast in the Jungle"? Sure of a negative answer, he goes on to support his position by quoting from Percy Lubbock's Introduction (1920) to the *Letters:*

In most lives experience is taken as it comes and left to rest in the memory where it happens to fall. Henry James never took anything as it came; the thing that happened to him was merely the point of departure for a deliberate, and as time went on a more and more masterly, creative energy . . . Looked at from without his life was uneventful enough, the even career of a man of letters, singularly fortunate in all its circumstances. Within, it was a cycle of vivid and incessant adventure . . .[3]

On that "cycle of vivid and incessant adventure" Edel takes his stand. Though outwardly serene, James lived intensely: "the thing that happened to him was merely the point of departure . . ."

What Edel fails to measure, however, is the significance of the cycle taking place "within." By using Lubbock, who in turn seems to be using "The Art of Fiction," Edel ends by defining James's experience as precisely a cerebral activity— what one does internally with one's impressions. I assent to this definition, but it seems to me to suggest through its "inwardness" the very possibility Edel denies: that Henry James's life was his art. That is, the isolated, cerebral experience of

2. Leon Edel, *The Untried Years* (Philadelphia: J. B. Lippincott, 1953), p. 13.
3. *Ibid.,* p. 14.

the man—the experience of imagining or observing relationships to be used in his art rather than of actively sharing in relationships with others—serves as a model for the characteristic experience of the heroes who people his art. Therefore, the drama of John Marcher, to whom nothing happens except "within," is disturbingly analogous to the drama of his creator.

James, of course, is perfectly aware of Marcher's failure to live; indeed, "one of the central recurring themes in . . . [his] novels is the desire to 'live,' to achieve . . . the richest . . . response to the vibrations of life."[4] But the failure to live at that ideal level, and the refusal to live at a lower one, are more profoundly characteristic of James's novels. The desire for human experience is doubled by the dread of human experience, and the only major character in the Jamesian world who can successfully mediate this paradox is the figure (regardless of his name) of the observer-artist. Physically passive and imaginatively bold, he attains only indirectly his own peculiar experience, an experience which is primarily psychic and dependent, in complex ways, upon the behavior of those whom he observes.

Such a character, I conclude, is fundamentally related to his creator: a fastidious man who avoids the vulgar exploitation of others common to the world of everyday relationships but who, through the shaping thrust of his imaginative inquiry, is exploitative nonetheless. More subtly than the man of experience, the detached observer-artist just as surely violates the privacy and integrity of others. Exploitation is inescapable in the Jamesian world, as present in those relationships founded on imagination as in those founded on intimacy and passion. To confess and mitigate such exploitation is the burden, early and late, of James's themes and forms.

In my different chapters I have focused on the desire to experience life more fully, either through contact with Euro-

---

4. Arnold Kettle, *An Introduction to the English Novel* (London: Hutchinson, 1953), II,33.

pean civilization or through an understanding of intimacy and passion. With one exception the contact was seen to be largely disillusioning; the understanding, frustrated or appalled. Moreover, in that exception—*The Golden Bowl*—the fusion of imagination and experience reveals, through its strain, the insurmountable discrepancy between ideal and actuality.

Yet there is a vast difference between the utterly defeated Rowland Mallet and the oddly triumphant Lambert Strether. I suggest that this is a difference caused by James's changing attitude toward the life of imagination. While Rowland chafes under the restrictions placed upon him by his role as vicarious observer, Strether settles with wit and ease into a similar part. While Rowland seeks Mary Garland, Strether seeks "not, out of the whole affair, to have got anything for myself." In other words, Rowland is condemned to a role of perception alone; Strether, finally, wants nothing else.

The formal changes in the novels of the nineties, as I argued in my chapter on *What Maisie Knew,* seem tailored for just such a character as Strether, for they inevitably emphasize vision to the exclusion of action. Focusing on the mind of an innocent protagonist, James works more with the process of perception than with the thing perceived, and in Strether he creates a hero who is more comfortable working the same way. Isolated, imaginative speculations about life tend increasingly to replace any active experience of it, or—it comes to this—the hero's experience of life is predominantly imaginative alone. Consequently, what was tragic in *The Portrait of a Lady*—the disparity between the imagined and the real—becomes tragicomic in *The Ambassadors:* Strether "all comically, all tragically"(II,327) chooses at the end to live with an imaginative vision of experience rather than engage more directly with such an experience itself.

The tragicomic poise embodied in Strether is precarious, however, for the relation between impoverished life and the active imagination is always potentially tragic in the Jamesian world. Life is inadequate to the hero's vision of it, and in his next novel, *The Wings of the Dove,* James focuses power-fully on the bitterness of that inadequacy. Then, as though once and for all to redress the failure to live (latent in all his imaginative characters) that culminates in Milly Theale, James writes *The Golden Bowl.* There the gap between the outside world and Maggie's vision of it is ultimately bridged by her imaginative power. Where Strether and Milly saw more than the actual case presented, Maggie succeeds in transform-ing the actual case, in creating "the bowl without the crack." But the substantial problems of *The Golden Bowl* stem precisely from the gap I have been tracing between actual and ideal relationships. The two have never been compatible in James, and, when he finally attempts to fuse them, the result is a novel at once triumphant, confusing, and grotesque.

Though the garnering of experience remains a "value" throughout James's career, and though his heroes seek either an encounter with the great world or the knowledge of intimacy and passion, they want these things only as projected—and sometimes only as encountered—by the imagination. Once the innocent imagination is disillusioned, it tends to become sus-picious, to become the imagination of disaster. Experience often is envisaged at first as ideal, and at last as sinister, cor-rupting, unreliable.

I suggest that this view of life underlies James's work from beginning to end, that his fiction exhibits a radical separation between actual, inadequate relations and ideal, impossible ones. The real experience of his heroes is the drama of their discovery of that separation, the drama of their illusions and their disil-lusionment; and this is a cerebral drama full of suffering and painful personal growth, but shared by no one else. Passion and intimacy are imagined, not encountered, by James's heroes, and it should be clear now that the protagonists in this respect imitate their creator, for in writing his fiction James, too, imagines but does not encounter these things. It is in this sense that, Edel notwithstanding, Henry James's life was his art, and that the intense but narrow experience in the one is paralleled by the intense but narrow experience in the other.

In the face of James's achievement it would be fatuous and shortsighted to cavil at his deficiencies. Furthermore, one needs to bear in mind the famous passage from "The Art of Fiction": "we must grant the artist his subject, his idea, his *donnée;* our criticism is applied only to what he makes of it."[5] It seems to me, however, that, admirable though this advice be, it is faintly tinged with special pleading and that James himself, in a later essay (1888) on Maupassant, writes from a more comprehensive and critical point of view:

> M. de Maupassant has simply skipped the whole reflective part of his men and women—that reflective part which governs conduct and character . . . For those who are conscious of this element in life, look for it and like it, the gap will appear to be immense. It will lead them to say, "No wonder you have a contempt if that is the way you limit the field. No wonder you judge people roughly if that is the way you see them. Your work, on your premisses, remains the admirable thing it is, but is your 'case' not adequately explained?"[6]

Few novelists have succeeded more masterfully than James in expressing, through his own work, what Maupassant ignores: "the whole reflective part . . . which governs conduct and character"; it is the special province and triumph of his fiction. But if one rereads the passage, substituting "human intimacy and passion" for James's phrase, one glimpses an area of life that James did not "simply skip," but one to which, with the most extensive ramifications, he closed the door. Always imagined, passion and intimacy are never experienced by the characters in his work, and for some readers the denial of life thereby implied will appear to be immense.

5. *Selected Literary Criticism: Henry James,* ed. Morris Shapira (London: Heinemann, 1963), p. 60.
6. *Ibid.,* p. 110.

In conclusion, the combination of generosity and judgment in James's assessment of Maupassant provides a fitting perspective to take on James's own slender though permanent art, his "obstinate finality."[7] For finally, as R. P. Blackmur says, "a man writes as he can"; and the words, though simple, reverberate in the mind. On reflection, they suggest to me not only the critic's ideal generosity toward his subject, but also—as the justification of his own work—the impossible, inescapable task of rightly fusing appreciation with analysis, of presenting both "the admirable thing it is" and the " 'case' . . . adequately explained."

7. James applied this phrase to himself in a famous letter to Henry Adams (1914) defending his recently published *Autobiography* and, in a larger sense, justifying his lifelong calling. Quoted from *The Letters of Henry James,* ed. Percy Lubbock (New York: Scribner's, 1920),II,361.

Index

203